THE IMPORTANCE OF EARLY LEARNING

Report by Sir Christopher Ball

MARCH 1994

RSA

The Royal Society for the encouragement of
Arts, Manufactures & Commerce

Founded in 1754

Foreword

This report presents a challenge to the nation – to parents, educators, employers, parliament – indeed to our society as a whole. It demonstrates the importance of early learning as a preparation for effective education to promote social welfare and social order, and to develop a worldclass workforce. It shows how countries benefit which provide good pre-school education for their children. It reveals the heavy price we have paid for failing to implement Mrs Thatcher's promise of nursery education for all in her White Paper of 1972. We agree that this must now be put right.

The report examines good practice in pre-school education. It finds that the key factors are a curriculum which encourages 'active learning', well trained staff of the highest quality, and the involvement of parents in a 'triangle of care'. Each requires attention. The existing pattern of provision in the UK is insufficient and not good enough. Other countries, heeding the evidence of research, are doing better.

The time is ripe for significant change. The Prime Minister has personally responded to the growing public concern about provision of nursery education. The report argues that this should be among our highest priorities. It squarely confronts the problem of resources, and offers a new and unexpected solution. We too believe that 'no child born after the year 2000 should be deprived of opportunity and support for effective early learning'.

The report, containing seventeen recommendations for action, is controversial and provocative. It will stimulate a wide-ranging and lively debate. But we hope that this will not delay an effective response from the Government and others to whom it is addressed. All children should be enabled to start right.

Baroness Faithfull
Oxford City Council
Children's Officer 1958-70,
Director of Social Services 1970-74
(retired 1974)

Sir Bryan Nicholson
Deputy President, CBI

Vivien Stern
Director, National Association
for the Care and Resettlement of
Offenders

Contents

The RSA   *back cover*

Acknowledgements

This report has not been easy to write. It would have been impossible without the help of many other people and the aid provided by earlier reports and papers. Indeed, much of what is written has been said before, and often, and well. Nonetheless, the responsibility for this report lies solely with the author.

But a particular debt of gratitude is owed to Professor Kathy Sylva, co-director of the RSA project (and author of appendices C and E), to Gillian Pugh, Chris Pascal, Joanna Foster, Philip Gammage, and Frances Moore, who read and criticised an early draft, to the members of the steering group (not all of whom have been able to endorse all parts of the report), and to those who funded and sponsored the RSA project:

> Bernard van Leer Foundation
> Corporation of London
> Esmée Fairbairn Charitable Trust
> Forte Plc
> Gloucestershire Training and Enterprise Council
> London East Training and Enterprise Council
> The Post Office.

I also thank my colleagues at the RSA, especially Lesley James and Peta Clark, who have worked so hard to ensure that the report was completed on time and in good order, and have corrected many flaws and errors within it.

More than is usually so, this report has relied on its predecessors. Indeed, a careful reader will observe that it sometimes pays them the most sincere form of flattery. While the references acknowledge the full range of publications referred to, consulted or used in the preparation of Start Right, it is only fair to list here – with heartfelt thanks – those which have been constant companions, sure guides and particularly valuable to me:

> Boyer, E. (1991) *Ready to Learn*
> –Department of Education and Science, (1990) *Starting with Quality* ◦ *Rumbold.*
> Early Years Curriculum Group (1989) *Early Childhood Education*
> Holtermann, S. (1992) *Investing in Young Children*
> Meade, A. (1988) *Education to be More*
> National Commission on Education (1993) *Learning to Succeed* –
>   (especially chapter 6: 'A Good Start in Education')
> Pugh, G. (Ed.). (1992) *Contemporary Issues in the Early Years* –
> Pugh, G. (1992) *An Equal Start for all our Children?*
> Rowan, P. (1992) *Ready for School*
> Sylva, K. and Moss, P. (1992) *Learning Before School*

Summary

'The dogmas of the quiet past are inadequate to the present. The occasion is piled high with difficulty and we must rise with the occasion. As our case is new, so we must think anew and act anew.'

(Abraham Lincoln)

A broken promise

This report presents a challenge to the nation – to parents, educators, employers, parliament – indeed to our society as a whole. It demonstrates the importance of early learning as a preparation for effective education to promote social welfare and social order, and to develop a world class workforce. It shows how countries benefit which provide good pre-school education for children. It reveals the heavy price we have paid for failing to implement Margaret Thatcher's promise of nursery education for all in her White Paper of 1972. And it offers practical proposals for putting things right.

The best investment

'Give me a child for the first seven years, and you may do what you like with it afterwards.'
Starting with this maxim, the report continues:

The Jesuits were right. The influence of early learning is so important that, if you give children a good start, there is much less risk of things going wrong later; but if you don't (and things do), it is very difficult and expensive to put them right. Prison doesn't work. Along with health care and parental education, investment in good early learning for all its children is arguably the best investment a nation can make. Why don't we?

The Government has claimed that
* adequate provision is available
* there is insufficient research evidence to prove the value of nursery learning
* it would cost too much to provide it.

This report provides evidence and argument to counter each of these claims – which are in part contradictory. The UK is close to the bottom of the European league for publicly-funded pre-school educational places for three- to four-year-olds. This means that those children who most need good early learning, and can benefit most from it, are least likely to experience it.

Three questions answered

Q. Does early learning matter?
A. Pre-school education pays.

Good pre-school education leads to immediate and lasting social and educational benefits for all children – especially those from disadvantaged backgrounds. Investment in high-quality and effective early education provides a worthwhile social and economic return to society. The latest finding is that 'over the lifetimes of the participants, the pre-school programme returns to the public an estimated $7.16 for every dollar invested'.

Q. What is the nature of good practice?
A. Quality counts.

Poor pre-school education is almost as little use to children as none at all. High-quality provision requires:
* the integration of education and care
* unified responsibility for provision
* targets for growth by a specified year
* effective and continuing training of early years teachers and carers
* an appropriate curriculum encouraging active learning and 'purposeful play'
* partnership between parents and educators
* adequate resources.

Q. How can a universal entitlement to good early learning be provided?

A. A new solution.

Funding seems to be the problem, but in reality it is a question of priorities. Pre-school education is –

* a good investment:- over time its value out weighs its cost
* a social priority:- like clean water, inoculation, free elections and parliament
* highly effective education:- so the educational budget should be rebalanced in favour of early learning.

The report proposes a new solution to the problem by raising the compulsory full-time schooling age from five to six and recycling the resources to provide free half-day early learning for all children aged three to five in an integrated context of extended day care.

Five major findings

Back to basics

Children's early learning is a distinct and fundamental phase of education providing an essential preparation for successful schooling and adult learning. Good houses need strong foundations. A well-educated society needs nursery schools.

The triangle of care

Parents, professionals and the community as a whole form a strong 'triangle of care', a partnership enabling children to enjoy a secure, warm and stimulating childhood. While each partner has a proper role, they share a common purpose – 'to restrain sometimes, encourage often, love always'.

Better practice

Since high-quality provision is essential to good practice in early learning, the principles of good practice set out in the report need to be incorporated in a new Code of Conduct, guaranteed through effective arrangements for quality assurance and systematically monitored across the whole range of the UK's diverse public and private provision.

Political will

It is possible to make progress. The UK can (and should) ensure that 'no child born after the year 2000 be deprived of opportunity and support for effective early learning'. Resources can be found. What has been lacking up to now is political will.

A National scandal?

The current situation is little short of a national scandal. We have neglected the needs of the most vulnerable members of society – young children (especially those from deprived or disadvantaged backgrounds). Since 1972 governments of both left and right have failed to implement Margaret Thatcher's promise. For nearly a generation large numbers of the nation's children have been deprived of the right start to their lives, and society has paid the price in terms of educational failure and waste, low skills, disaffection and delinquency.

Seventeen recommendations

The report contains seventeen recommendations, addressed to parliament, educators, parents and the community, and the Government, including the following:

Parliament, political parties, parents, employers, the media, the churches and other voluntary, community and religious organisations should consider whether the provision for pre-school education in the UK is seriously inadequate, and take steps to persuade the Government to undertake an urgent review and act on its recommendations (Recommendation 4).

The churches, religious and community leaders should stimulate a major public debate on the subject of parenthood in order to establish exemplifications of good practice based on research and proven experience (Recommendation 5).

Professional bodies and institutions of training concerned with early childhood care and education should review their training and practice to ensure that they offer parents a real partnership (Recommendation 7).

The RSA and other bodies should pursue the issues of:
* the education and support of parents
* paid parental leave
* the care of pre-school children of those in employment

(Recommendation 11).

The Government should immediately prepare legislation to create by 1999 a statutory responsibility for the provision of free, high-quality, half-day pre-school education for all children from the age of three, in an integrated context of extended day-care (Recommendation 12).

The Department for Education should give consideration to raising the age at which children begin compulsory full-time schooling from five to six, and transferring the resources released thereby to enable pre-school education (as defined in recommendation 12) to be made available for all children aged three to five inclusive (Recommendation 13).

There should be **a public debate** of whether pre-school education should be made compulsory (Recommendation 14).

Do what is right

None of these things will happen without an assertion of political will, accompanied by popular support and directed through decisive leadership. The translation of national aspirations into reality cannot be achieved by government alone. It requires the co-operation, effort and enterprise of many agencies and all parts of society. Political will inevitably reflects the general will of society. But political leadership can shape the general will. Progress is possible. Nations have learned to free slaves, end child labour, extend the franchise to women. We can decide to stop neglecting the early education of our children. We may expect a range of economic, social and personal benefits if we do so. But these are not the most compelling reasons for action. We should act because it is right. Our children's children will not readily forgive us, if we decline to face the challenge, or fail.

1. The Case for Early Learning: a Vision for the Future

'Give me a child for the first seven years, and you may do what you like with it afterwards.'

(Jesuit maxim)

This chapter summarises the case for the systematic public provision of high quality pre-school education. Claims that adequate provision is already available, that the research is inconclusive, or that nursery education cannot be afforded, are refuted. In addition to the economic arguments, educational, social and moral reasons are presented for providing all children with the 'right start' to life. A range of impediments to progress is set out, but not found to be insurmountable. Four things are needed: a national system of paid parental leave, effective arrangements for the care of pre-school-age children of those in employment, the education and support of parents, and an entitlement to good early learning for all children from the age of three. The RSA project is focused on the fourth of these. All children should be enabled to start right. Thanks to the growing public awareness of the issue, and the Prime Minister's personal interest, this may soon be possible.

Starting right

1.1   The Jesuits were right. The influence of early learning* is so important that, if you give children a good start, there is much less risk of things going wrong later; but if you don't (and things do), it is very difficult and expensive to put them right. Prison doesn't work. Along with health care and parental education, investment in good early learning for all its children is arguably the best investment a nation can make. Why don't we?

The Government has claimed that
* adequate provision is available
* there is insufficient research evidence to prove the value of nursery learning
* it would cost too much to provide it.

This report provides evidence and argument to counter each of these claims – which are in part contradictory. The UK is close to the bottom of the European league for publicly-funded pre-school educational places for three- to four-year-olds. This means that those children who most need good early learning and can benefit most from it, are least likely to experience it.

1.2   Research in America shows that, for every 100 disadvantaged youngsters with good pre-school (nursery) education, 48 managed to gain employment, and 45 were able to support

---

    * See Appendix E for a glossary of key terms used throughout the report.

themselves completely on their own earnings, when they grew up; while for every 100 without pre-school education the comparable figures were 29 and 24. The latest finding is that 'over the lifetimes of the participants, the pre-school program returns to the public an estimated $7.16 for every dollar invested' (see Chapter 2 and appendices C and D). Far from costing too much, this is an opportunity we cannot afford to miss.

1.3   Current policy is pointing us in the wrong direction. The combination of a squeeze on public funding and the discretionary nature of nursery provision is leading some Local Education Authorities to reduce nursery places and close schools. The new proposals for Initial Teacher Training devalued 'early years' teachers. And the increase in admission of four-year-olds to primary schools may be doing more harm than good, if thereby they are being introduced to Key Stage 1 of the National Curriculum too early – and taught by teachers not trained to work with this age-group.

1.4   Good early learning must be appropriate to the developmental stage of three- and four-year-olds, allowing them to explore the varieties of intelligence and styles of learning through purposeful play. One of the major findings of research is that the payback on investment in early learning is directly related to the quality of the provision. This will seem like common sense to the myriad of middle-class parents who can afford to pay for good nursery places – and observe the consequential benefits in their children's later successes in learning, life and work.

1.5   In addition to the economic argument there are three compelling reasons why it is essential to provide the 'right start' for all children for the future. The first is educational. Good early learning leads to later educational success; it significantly reduces the risk of disaffection, drop-out and failure. The American High/Scope study reveals that 71% of those on good pre-school programmes completed 12th grade (or better), as compared with 54% of those denied it. A well-controlled British study showed that children who have experienced pre-school education have higher scores on educational assessment at the age of seven (Shorrocks, 1992)*. According to the National Commission, 'pupils' early attainment at school is a good indicator of later educational success, and perhaps a more reliable indicator than family background' (see appendix G). This should be no surprise, since it is known that humans learn fastest and most effectively in the early years.

1.6   The second reason is social. Good early learning socialises young people; it reduces the risk of later juvenile delinquency. The same American study shows that good pre-school programmes led to significantly fewer arrests up to the age of 27 (e.g. 7% in comparison with 35%, with five or more arrests; 7%, against 25%, involved with crimes associated with drugs). Together with parental education, the provision of good early learning is arguably the best available means to tackle crime. Prevention works better than cure.

1.7   The third reason is one of equity – both justice for children and equitable treatment of parents. As far as is possible, all children should be enabled to start the adventure of education from the same point. And all parents should have equal access to employment. But it is not just a question of equity; it also derives from economic need. The provision of equal opportunities in work requires a system of paid parental leave and extended daycare for infants, if women are to be enabled to take and retain their place in the workforce. And we need them. Some 80% of the new jobs likely to be created before the end of the century are

---

*   Shorrocks, D., Daniels, S., Frobisher, L., Nelson, N., Waterson, A. & Bell, J. (1992) ENCA 1 Project: The Evaluation of National Curriculum Assessment at Key Stage 1.

expected to be filled by women. The challenge is to find a way *both* of releasing parents to join the workforce *and* of ensuring high quality care for their children, enriched by the encouragement of early learning. The entitlement to good nursery education from the age of three offers the best answer to a major part of that challenge. But parents – of both genders – also need to be able to take a period of about six months of paid leave on the birth of a child, followed by access to good quality extended daycare, for which they can be expected to pay on a means-tested basis, if they are in employment.

Impediments to progress

1.8   So what are the problems? Despite Margaret Thatcher's recognition, when she was Secretary of State for Education in 1972, that all children would benefit from nursery education, government policies (or rather the lack of a comprehensive government policy – and commitment to it) stand in the way of progress. The absence of a single department with overall responsibility for children under five, and the divisions between the Education and Health Departments, do not help. (Scotland, with a less divided system of government than England, has a somewhat better record.) The Department for Education appears reluctant to be convinced that pre-school education is a desirable and necessary investment. In consequence, the public services that exist are discretionary – and vulnerable to cuts when public expenditure is squeezed.

1.9   There is no 'specific grant' for early learning, and Local Authorities have no duty to provide it. Nursery education must therefore compete for resources with all other areas of local government responsibility, such as libraries, adult education, or services for old people. While the current Standard Spending Assessments are now so much reduced that cuts in discretionary services (like childcare and nursery education) are inevitable, the most serious problem arises from the system for distributing local government finance, which penalises authorities which choose to make more than an average level of provision. Although both the Home Office and Employment Department are showing a developing interest in early learning and nursery education, recent legislation, from the Education Reform Act 1988 to the Education Act of 1992, and consequential regulations, have ignored pre-school learning and made changes (e.g. to the role of Local Authorities, provision for 'opted-out' schools, the inspection services, initial teacher training) which have further weakened what was already an inadequate provision.

1.10   Although the situation is gradually changing, the general public does not yet view the provision of good early learning for all children as an urgent, important or high-priority issue. One measure of its neglect is the different levels of funding provided for pupils and students as they progress towards maturity. Recent figures from New Zealand, which are not untypical for the pattern of provision in other developed countries, show that the relative proportions for the annual costs of (a) pre-school and primary, (b) secondary pupils, (c) higher education and teacher training are (a) 2, (b) 3, (c) 8. In the UK, a primary school child is 'worth' £1350, a secondary child £2030, and a university student about £4800. The public appears to condone this absurd inequity. Current plans for the resourcing of grant-maintained schools by means of a 'Common Funding Formula' would make matters still worse. A second measure is the low employment status of carers and early-years teachers. The argument that 'anyone can teach and care for young children competently, because most people do so as parents' is as fallacious as a claim that 'anyone can drive cars competently, because most of us do so'. It overlooks the need for the competence derived from training, assessment and qualification. But, above all, it misses the point of quality: the professionalism of good carers and teachers – and the corresponding competence of parents – lies in the *high quality* of the education and care that is provided by them.

1.11 Public neglect of the challenge of early learning has many causes. Some have argued that there is (at least in England) a lack of interest in, and commitment to, education that is culturally distinctive and well characterised by Lord Melbourne's celebrated remark to Queen Victoria: 'I don't know, Ma'am, why they make all this fuss about education: none of the Pagets can read or write, and they get on well enough'. Others observe that, not only do young children lack a voice (and a vote), but their parents are typically young adults with limited influence and political experience. But perhaps the most significant issue is our national tradition of respecting the privacy of family life and delaying intervention until the moment of crisis.

1.12 John Bowlby's work on child development published in the middle of the century has tended to reinforce this national attitude. Bowlby constructed an ethological theory which asserted the biological basis of early emotional attachments. He argued that both mother and baby are genetically programmed to seek contact with one another. From this, a deep emotional bond was thought to develop which (if broken by even brief separation) led to serious distress for both child and mother. These ideas have dominated our understanding of child development – and of family relationships – for about 50 years. They have provided an apparently scientific basis for popular views, such as 'a mother's place is in the home' or 'fathers cannot be adequate parents for small children' or 'childcare and early learning separate from the mother may be harmful'. Bowlby's early views have been challenged and were in any event modified later (see *Suggested Reading* for published critiques). Current research suggests that before the age of one children bond with a limited number of adults. For this reason it may well be that they will thrive best in a home environment. Fathers can be as competent parents as mothers, if they (both) learn the job properly. There is no good evidence to support the view that daycare or centre-based learning for children (at least over the age of one) is harmful, and there is growing evidence that, provided it is of good quality, it is beneficial. (The evidence of research for the first year is conflicting.)

1.13 The importance of Bowlby's ideas (and of their later revision) is profound. Many of those who hold power and influence have been impressed and conditioned by simplified versions of his earlier claims. Decision-makers in our society are still mostly men: as such they are less likely either to have experienced a direct need for childcare or to have a personal interest in the issues involved with it. Conversely, those who are expert in childcare or pre-school education rarely achieve positions of power and influence. It is notable that the new positive policy on early learning and childcare in New Zealand was developed at a time when the Prime Minister was also Minister of Education, and his chief adviser an early childhood specialist. The same pattern obtains at a local level. Since services are discretionary, positive policies depend on the political will and commitment of elected members and their senior officers. It is hardly surprising that the level of provision and quality vary markedly from locality to locality. Nonetheless, local government – which tends to involve a higher proportion of women than central government – has significantly led the way in seeking to provide high-quality care and education for young children.

1.14 Just as the level and quality of childhood services vary, so does the quality of parenting that children receive. It is difficult to exaggerate the value of committed parents and good parenting skills. They are even more important to a child's lifelong welfare than good nursery and primary education. Parents need support and education of two kinds: in understanding the long term and serious demands of the role, and in the acquisition of the relevant skills. The trouble is that some people have allowed themselves to believe that one of our essential liberties is the freedom to be ignorant, incompetent and downright bad parents. This mistaken and harmful belief arises from the idea that it is possible to have rights without corresponding obligations. The right to parenthood implies the obligation to seek to be a good parent. Can parental skills be taught effectively within the National Curriculum? Perhaps the right to child benefit should also incur the obligation to undertake parental training? This is a difficult and controversial area. But one of the impediments to progress in the provision of good early learning for all children is the absence of a shared understanding of the nature of the 'social contract'. In this respect, it is worth noting that the Children Act 1989 marked a significant change in establishing the rights of children and the responsibilities of parents. However, subsequent educational legislation continues to refer to parental rights – and ignores those of children. This report seeks throughout to address issues from the point of view of the interests of children – and makes the fundamental assumption that the rights of the child are paramount.

1.15 Until recently, the 'early childhood profession' has failed to speak with one voice. Different groups have emphasised different arguments for improved provision, contrasting (for example) the needs of mothers with the benefits for children; or they appear to have different aims, opposing the creation of a safety net for vulnerable families to the provision of a better start for all children. The diversity of services which already exist includes nursery schools, playgroups, family centres and childminders. It will not be easy to provide a systematic universal entitlement to early learning which unites the various strengths of the diverse forms of existing provision, and avoids their weaknesses, without threatening the status quo in some respects at least. Children need to be able to learn in the care of teams which are professionally led – and are also trained to support, develop and work alongside parents. All concerned should understand the process and curriculum of early learning, the importance of keeping records of children's development, and the need to ensure seamless progression from babyhood in the home (or in daycare) through the experience of early learning into the National Curriculum (Key Stage 1) in the primary school. Easier said than done. Early childhood educators, in particular, have been reluctant to fight for better pay, improved conditions of service, or higher status. They have not yet formed an effective pressure group or learned the arts of political persuasion. Perhaps they should recall both halves of the biblical injunction: 'Be ye therefore wise as serpents, and harmless as doves'.

1.16 Lastly, both sides of the 'cost-effectiveness' equation create impediments to progress. With the existing national budgetary deficit, it is probably unrealistic to expect a substantial increase in real terms in the funds available for education for some years. But it is to be hoped that (if they cannot be increased) resources can at least be maintained at their present level, and that the balance of funding can be tilted in favour of early learning. This may mean persuading other parts of the education system to release resources – which is unlikely to be easy. Standards of nursery education are high in the UK and good quality childcare is not cheap. The temptation to trade off quality against quantity of provision must be resisted, however, because the evidence for the benefit of early learning shows that it depends critically on the quality of the provision.

The promised land

1.17   Those who are marching to the Promised Land have little hope of safe arrival without a map of the route and a sketch of the objective. In this report, Chapter 7 is intended to serve for the map. What is the aim? What would success look like? Four things are needed to give every child a fair chance of starting right:

a) a national system of paid parental leave,
b) effective arrangements for the care of the (pre-school age) children of those in employment,
c) the education and support of parents, and
d) an entitlement to good early learning for all children from the age of three.

Since the emphasis of this report is upon early learning, and its focus on the needs of the child, it is the fourth of these that predominates – though the third is also discussed, especially in Chapter 5. The others have been thoroughly explored elsewhere★. All four are necessary and give support to one another. It will not be enough to introduce parental education without providing for paid parental leave, for example, (or vice versa); or to offer childcare to those who are in employment without consideration of the role of early learning (or, again, vice versa). However, the definition of the promised land for the RSA project is that no child born after the year 2000 in the UK should be deprived of opportunity and support for effective early learning. All children should be enabled to start right.

1.18   This may soon be possible. The strength of the case for the provision of early learning is becoming apparent. The impediments standing in the way of progress are no longer seen to be immovable. In particular, as the report argues, the resource constraints can be overcome. But, even more important than these considerations, there is a growing social awareness of the importance of early learning and pre-school education. The media are alive to the issue. Whatever is meant by 'back to basics' it must include parental competence and pre-school provision. And, once raised into public consciousness, the question is unlikely to fade away until it has been satisfactorily resolved. The masterly and influential report of the National Commission on Education, *Learning to Succeed* (1993) has proposed as its Goal No. 1 that 'high quality nursery education must be available for all three- and four-year-olds' (see appendix G of this report which reproduces Chapter 6, 'A Good Start in Education'). This report concurs.

1.19   Many other nations are acting on the assumption that the benefits of early learning have been demonstrated. For example, India has given priority to the provision of early education and childcare by transferring funding from higher education. Just as the UK seems to be almost the only country still debating whether 'learning pays', so few other nations are questioning the value of early learning today. It is encouraging that, after a careful review, the House of Commons Select Committee on Education reported in 1989: 'we conclude from the evidence that education for under fives can effectively contribute to the various social, educational and compensatory objectives set out in the 1972 White Paper. It can not only enrich the child's life at the time but can also prepare the child for the whole process of schooling'. The most hopeful sign, however, is the interest and concern of the Prime Minister, expressed in frequent public statements in recent months.

★ For example, in the Equal Opportunity Commission's discussion paper: *The Key to Real Choice, an action plan for childcare* (1990).

2. The Evidence of Research

'The benefits of complementary early childhood care and education are proven without doubt by research and experience'

(Anne Meade, 1988, *Education to be More*)

This chapter summarises the evidence of research (which is set out more fully in appendix C). It concludes that published research on the value of, and good practice in, the provision of early learning (though somewhat sparse and problematic) is yet reliable and decisive. It demonstrates the effectiveness of high quality pre-school education in providing both social and educational benefits. The impact is strongest in children from disadvantaged backgrounds. Active learning is the key to success. Good early learning improves aspiration, motivation, socialisation and self-esteem. It thereby develops 'mastery', without which successful schooling and adult learning is unlikely. Investment in high-quality early education provides a worthwhile economic return to society. There are two recommendations on the need for, and nature of, further research.

Introduction

2.1 We don't need research to remind us of the importance of good parental care for young children. Nor of the advantages they gain from books in the home, opportunities for constructive play, encouragement to ask and answer questions, shared experience, or a framework of moral discipline. These things are obvious. And few doubt the value of primary and secondary education – which is why most nations (that can afford it) require by statute, and make provision for, all children to receive some ten years of full-time education. The United Nations Convention on the Rights of the Child recognises the right to education: ratifying nations are to 'make primary education compulsory and available free to all'. The question is whether there are further significant benefits for children in the experience of early learning outside the home before the statutory age for school entry. This report offers an affirmative answer based on reliable research.

2.2 'Centre-based' early learning comes in several forms: nursery schools, nursery and reception classes (in primary schools), day nurseries, combined nursery centres, childcare centres, family centres, and playgroups. It can be provided by the State, voluntary bodies or private education. This diversity of provision instantly complicates the task of research, and qualifies its findings. Similarly, other nations make different dispositions: for example, the statutory age for entry to full-time education (five in the UK) is elsewhere usually six, and sometimes seven. Before the evidence of research can be confidently applied, it is essential to ensure that like is compared with like, and that contexts are sufficiently similar to justify the assumption that findings are transferable.

2.3 Scepticism about the research evidence for the importance of early learning arises from several sources. One is ignorance – which may in part be dispelled by this report. Another is the long chain of causality between, for example, the nursery school and adult earnings. A third is the complexity of benefit (both cognitive and social) derived from good early learning. A fourth is the important qualification contained in the phrase 'good early learning': the benefits are related to the quality. A fifth is the differential benefit for children from disadvantaged homes: all children benefit, but those whose needs are greatest gain most. A sixth relates to the prospects for payback: can it be demonstrated that investment in high-quality early education provides a worthwhile economic return? A seventh is a suspicion that educational research of this nature may lack scientific rigour. Finally, there is a widespread perception (shared by both researchers and their critics) that the available research is barely adequate – in quantity, scope, depth and extent – to provide reliable evidence. Each of these problems is squarely addressed in Professor Sylva's authoritative paper (appendix C), and dealt with in summary fashion in what follows. It is interesting that schools, colleges and universities are rarely required to prove their value in such terms. No doubt they could. But it is the contention of this report that the lasting value of education can most clearly be demonstrated for early learning – not least through its effect of enhancing the value of later childhood and adult education.

Effectiveness

2.4   Both in the USA and the UK there has been the same interesting sequence of events over the past 25 years or so: (a) significant intervention with new programmes of early learning aimed at 'breaking the cycle of poverty' or 'closing the poverty gap'; (b) initial evaluations, which reported that gains in intelligence tended to disappear after a few years; (c) subsequent more sophisticated re-evaluation, which reported a wider range of benefits – and some evidence that they persist into adult life.

2.5   How is this to be explained? There seem to be two main reasons for this apparent contradiction. First, the relative rigour of the research is significant. Where the programmes were rigorously designed (to take account, for example, of parental choice) and carefully controlled (with matched groups of children) the benefits are most clear. Secondly, the cumulative evidence on the importance of early learning enables a more precise claim to be made: that the beneficial impact of early learning is (a) related to the quality of provision, (b) strongest in children from disadvantaged backgrounds, and (c) as much concerned with self-esteem and social cohesion as with cognitive development. Programmes of research which fail to recognise these three important qualifications are of less value in measuring effectiveness than those which do. Each is dealt with in turn below (2.10 – 2.19).

2.6   One of the most carefully controlled programmes of intervention in the USA was the Perry Pre-School Project, later known as High/Scope. The curriculum is of outstanding quality; staff are well trained; parental participation is encouraged. (In fact, the curriculum is similar to [and shares common roots with] much high-quality British nursery education – which strengthens the relevance of this research for the UK.) The programme has been carefully evaluated over 30 years and has consistently shown striking results. Although the initial gains in intelligence tests had disappeared by the secondary school stage, there were remarkable differences in outcome between the 65 children who attended the half-day educational programme over two years and the control group of 58 children who remained at home. Figures 1 and 2 present in graphic form the long-term effects of the programme.

Figure 1. High/Scope Perry Preschool study. Effects of the programme at age 27.

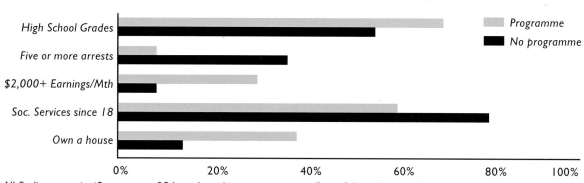

All findings are significant at p<.05 based on chi-square statistics. From Schweinhart and Weikart (1993).

Figure 2. High/Scope Perry Preschool study. Sources of public costs and benefits per participant. From Schweinhart and Weikart (1993)

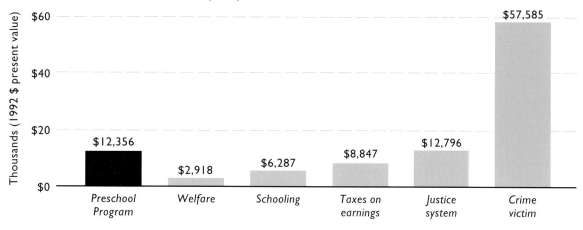

In summary, by the age of 27 the High/Scope 'pre-school graduate' had
* higher monthly earnings (29% vs 7% earning $2,000 or more per month)
* higher percentage of home ownership (36% vs 13%) and of second car ownership (30% vs 13%)
* a higher level of schooling completed (71% vs 54% completing 12th grade or higher)
* a lower percentage receiving social services at some time in the past ten years (59% vs 80%)
* fewer arrests (7% vs 35% with five or more), including fewer arrested for crimes of drug taking or dealing (7% vs 25%).

Throughout the course of the longitudinal study of the effects of the High/Scope programme researchers found markedly different (and better) educational performances in the pre-school programme participants. In particular, the programme groups produced significantly higher scores than the control group in tests of:
a) intellectual performance from the end of the first year of the pre-school programme to the end of first grade at the age of seven;
b) school achievement at the age of 14;
c) general literacy at the age of 19.

The latest findings of the significant benefits of High/Scope are so impressive that they have been included as appendix D to this report.

2.7   However, Margaret Clark's review of British research on the effects of pre-school attendance tells a rather different story (Clark, 1988, *Children Under Five: educational research and education*). She reviewed all the major British research studies on enrolment, characteristics of provision, curriculum, special needs, continuity into school, and many other topics. Although her thorough review covered small-scale studies as well as large ones, it led to few firm conclusions. She observed that:

a) most studies showed that attendance at pre-school of some kind was associated with positive benefits for the children;

b) many early benefits were not seen to last beyond the infant school;

c) it was not yet possible to know which kinds of provision brought about the most successful outcome.

Clark particularly emphasised the need for more and better qualitative and quantitative research.

2.8   The difficulty of evaluating research on early learning can be seen clearly in the analysis of three relevant studies in appendix C. The Child Health and Educational Study of some 8,400 children born in 1970[*] showed a clear association between pre-school attendance and both educational outcomes (improved literacy and numeracy) and social development (reduced behavioural problems) at the age of ten. But this undoubted correlation cannot safely be interpreted as cause and effect, because of the lack of matched samples of children at the point of entry. Similarly, neither of two conflicting studies which investigated possible links between nursery attendance and performance in the Standard Assessment Tasks can be relied upon for detailed policy decision, because both studies depended on the teachers of the seven-year-old children to distinguish those who had attended nursery from those who had not. Teachers identified more than half as having attended 'nursery', while government statistics show the figure for Local Education Authority nurseries to be more like 25%. It is clear that other forms of provision must have been included.

2.9   While further rigorous research is undoubtedly required, the evidence from many research studies justifies the firm conclusion that pre-school education leads to immediate, measurable gains in educational and social development. Although the High/Scope project is the most complete longitudinal study available, its findings and implications are confirmed by other research, and are gradually receiving endorsement from other countries. For example, research in France has shown that attendance at nursery school is associated with better progress in primary education, in as much as the proportion required to 'repeat a year' is substantially higher for those without nursery experience (Jarousse and Mingat, 1991, *La sociologie de l'école*).

Quality

2.10   Quality matters. The evidence shows that it is *high quality* early education that leads to lasting cognitive and social benefits in children. What does quality consist in? It seems to be critically linked to three major factors – the early-learning curriculum, the selection, training and continuity of staff, and staff:children ratios – and also to be associated (but less critically) with three other factors – the buildings and equipment of the early learning centre and the

---

[*] Osborn, A. F. & Millbank, J. E. (1987) The effects of early education: a report from the Child Health (1992) *Contemporary Issues in the Early Years*

role of parents. Some British research has been directed towards evaluating the relative merits of different kinds of provision (daycare versus nursery education, for example), with ambiguous results. Research from other countries shows that it is the quality, rather than the type, of provision that is most important.

2.11 In the USA a group of researchers studied the effects of three different curricula: a High/Scope 'purposeful play' programme, a 'free play' programme and a formal pre-school curriculum. (Schweinhart, Weikart and Larner, 1986, *Consequences of three pre-school curriculum models through age 15*). Children in all three groups showed gains in intelligence at school entry. However, a follow-up study at the age of fifteen revealed that the children who had attended the formal programmes showed more anti-social behaviour and had a lower commitment to school than those who had attended the two programmes based on play. This research demonstrates a link between an active learning programme before school entry and lasting benefits in the form of increased confidence and maturity in adolescence.

2.12 In the UK a research study examined two matched groups of 45 children starting primary school: one group had experienced state nursery education, the other voluntary playgroups (Jowett and Sylva, 1986, *Does Kind of Pre-School Matter?*). Earlier research had shown significant curricular difference between the two types of provision in the examples studied. The study found that the children who had attended nurseries engaged in more purposeful and complex play in the reception class of primary school than did those who had attended playgroups. During 'free choice' sessions, the nursery children were more 'learning oriented'. Figure 3 presents evidence to show that the nursery children were more persistent and independent when they encountered obstacles. This study, demonstrating the relative effectiveness of different types of pre-school provision, suggests that the critical factors lie in the curriculum and (no doubt) the selection and training of staff.

Figure 3. Reactions to children's task difficulty.
From Jowett and Sylva (1986)

Term	Group	Asks for help %	Gives up %	Persists %
Autumn	Nursery N=78	17	1	82
	Playgroup N=77	36	22	42
Summer	Nursery N=63	14	17	68
	Playgroup N=37	49	30	22

2.13 Similarly, studies of the effects of learning within a daycare setting repeatedly emphasise the significance of quality. There is disagreement among scholars as to whether early entry to daycare (i.e. before the age of one) is harmful to children's later development. The question, though important, is not germane to this report – which is concerned with evaluating the benefits of 'centre-based' early learning from the age of three, on the assumption that good parental practice will provide either home-based early learning before the age of three or high-quality daycare (where needed) for one- and two-year-olds. Studies from the USA, the UK and Sweden all tend to show that, provided it is of high quality, the provision of early learning (after the age of one) in a daycare setting does not harm children's emotional, social or educational development, and may well give them a better start in life. For example, Howes (1990) *Can the Age of Entry into Child Care and the Quality of Child Care Predict Adjustment in Kindergarten?* studied 80 children in matched groups experiencing high- and low-quality daycare. Not surprisingly, the former group did better when they entered school, both educationally and socially. The characteristics of the high-quality daycare centres included: (a) stable childcare arrangements, (b) low staff turnover, (c) good staff training in child development, (d) low adult:child ratios (e.g. for one- to three-year-olds, 1:4; for four- to six-year-olds, 1:8 to 1:12).

Disadvantage

2.14   While all children benefit from the provision of opportunities for high-quality early learning, the effects are strongest in those from disadvantaged backgrounds. In many evaluative studies of pre-school education, it has been shown that 'pre-school intervention is particularly effective for the most economically disadvantaged children' (Zigler, 1987, *Formal Schooling for Four-Year-Olds?: No*). For example, a particularly interesting and well-designed study of the American Head Start programme managed to separate the effects of race from those of initial test scores (Lee, Brooks-Gunn and Schnur, 1988)★. It demonstrated that black children gained more than white ones, and black children of below-average ability gained more than their peers of average ability. The study concludes 'that those black students who exhibited the greatest cognitive disadvantage at the outset appeared to benefit most from Head Start participation'. It is also noteworthy that the study of the High/Scope programme shows stronger benefits for girls than for boys. If we seek to close the gap (or break the cycle) of poverty, inequality and deprivation, good early learning for the mothers of tomorrow is likely to make a significant difference.

2.15   The finding that the impact of early education is strongest in disadvantaged children must be applied with care. It does not justify a selective and separate provision for such children, since there is considerable evidence that the concentration of children with behavioural or learning difficulties in one centre does little to help them. The ghetto-effect provides yet another disadvantage. This analysis helps to explain the contrasting evidence on daycare from Sweden and the UK (see appendix C). From this it is possible to devise a further important feature of high-quality provision; namely the quality, diversity and range of the peer-group. It appears to be as important a factor in early learning as it has long been understood to be in secondary or higher education.

Self-esteem and social cohesion

2.16   The most important learning in pre-school education has to do with aspiration, socialisation and self-esteem. The art of learning is not a mystery. No-one learns effectively without motivation, social skills and confidence – and very few fail to learn successfully if they have developed these enabling attitudes and 'super skills' of learning. They lie at the heart of the early-learning curriculum. The second great commandment teaches us to love our neighbours as ourselves; more concisely, elegantly and memorably than modern jargon can, these

---

★   Lee, V. Brooks-Gunn, J. & Schnur, E. (1988). *Does Head-Start Work?* A one year follow-up comparison of disadvantaged children attending Head-Start, no pre-school, and other pre-school programmes. Developmental Psychology, 24 (2), pp.210-222

words identify the fundamental importance of self-esteem and social cohesion for the well-lived life. They are also essential for successful learning.

2.17   Modern educational research is on the threshold of a revolution. The findings of brain-science, for example, or the theory of multiple intelligence, or the idea of different styles of learning, or the recognition that people can learn to learn faster, are all pointing the way towards a new and powerful theory of learning which will be able to satisfy the three tests of explanation, prediction and application. Central to the new theory will be a clearer understanding of learning development, and the sequence whereby people progress from infancy to become mature learners. In the (recent) past the professionalism of teachers has often been thought to reside in mastering the subject or discipline. But these are merely the tokens of learning. The art of learning (learning how to learn) is also concerned with the types, or 'super skills' and attitudes, of learning – of which motivation, socialisation and confidence are the most important. These are the fruits of successful early learning.

2.18   Professor Sylva outlines in appendix C an explanatory account of how good early education does much more than merely instil a few facts or teach simple cognitive skills. The High/Scope curriculum (for example), built on the 'plan, do, review' cycle, encourages 'mastery' learning. There appear to be two interesting patterns of behaviour shown by children (and adults) when they experience difficulties, problems or failure. 'Helpless' children avoid challenge, give up easily and tend to despise themselves; 'Mastery' children enjoy challenge, persevere and trust in their own competence – even in the face of obstacles. These patterns of behaviour are not related to intelligence or innate ability: they are features of character or personality – and they can be learned or unlearned. They appear to be in part determined by choice of goals. 'Helpless' children seek rewards from adults (e.g. high marks in school); 'mastery' children pursue goals of learning and discovery for their own sake. There is also a significant link between 'mastery' orientation and a belief (in both children and parents) that effort can lead to increased intelligence. By contrast, 'helpless' children (and their parents) tend to maintain a naive version of IQ theory – that those of high intelligence don't need to work hard, and those of low intelligence will fail however hard they try.

2.19   The importance of these ideas for the understanding and explanation of later educational success and failure is obvious. Early learning, properly understood, provides a foundation stage upon which successful schooling and adult learning can be built. Without this stage in place, those of a 'helpless' orientation develop and continue patterns of behaviour which disable them – and which are difficult to correct once they become fixed. Good early learning encourages 'mastery'. It is significant that the outcome-related National Vocational Qualifications/Scottish Vocational Qualifications (NVQs/SVQs) also emphasise 'mastery learning'. If the National Targets for Education and Training , which are mostly expressed and measured in NVQs/SVQs, are to be reached by the year 2000 and surpassed in the 21st century, then it will be necessary to encourage 'mastery learning' in as many as possible in each successive age-cohort. Systematic provision for good early learning will enable this to happen.

Payback

2.20   Finally, there remains the question of payback. Can it be demonstrated that investment in high-quality early education provides a worthwhile economic return? Yes. The evidence of the value of High/Scope (see 2.6) indicated not only an improvement in the quality of life of the participants, but also significant economic benefits for society. A cost-benefit analysis has estimated that for every $1,000 invested in the pre-school programme (after adjustment for inflation) at least $7,160 has been, or will be, returned to society. These calculations were based on the reduced costs of juvenile delinquency, remedial education, income support and unemployment (resulting from the beneficial effect of High/Scope) set against the costs of their high quality pre-school programme. Society also benefits from the higher taxes contributed from the increased earnings of 'pre-school graduates' who thus play a part in raising Gross Domestic Product. It is striking that the rate of return has increased as the participants have matured, and the costs of crime and welfare have entered the picture. At the age of eight, the return was calculated to be $2 for every $1 invested; at fifteen, it was $4; at nineteen, $6; and by the age of 27 it has risen to just over $7. There have been further studies involving cost-benefit analysis of pre-school programmes in the US (see appendix C): they show that the costs of the programmes were more than offset by later savings in the children's educational and medical care. Early learning pays.

Conclusions

2.21   This summary review of the evidence of research, together with the more elaborate account provided by Professor Sylva in appendix C, justifies the following *conclusions*:

a) pre-school education leads to immediate, measurable gains in educational and social development;

b) early education leads to lasting cognitive and social benefits in children, provided it is of high quality (defined in terms of (i) a curriculum based on the principle of active learning or 'purposeful play', (ii) the selection, training, retention and ratio of staff, (iii) parental involvement (iv) buildings and equipment, (v) diversity of the peer group);

c) while all the children benefit, the impact of early education is strongest in children from disadvantaged backgrounds;

d) as a consequence of b) i and ii, neither voluntary playgroups nor early entry to primary education and to Key Stage I of the National Curriculum (in their present form) is a suitable alternative to high-quality pre-school education;

e) active and responsible learning is the key to the success of the most effective programmes;

f) the most important learning in pre-school education has to do with aspiration, motivation, socialisation and self-esteem;

g) good early learning encourages and develops 'mastery' without which successful schooling and adult learning is unlikely;

h) investment in high-quality early education provides a worthwhile economic return to society.

2.22   While these conclusions are secure, and the research on which they are based is reliable, the quantity, scope, depth and extent of available research (especially in the UK) do not yet reflect the importance of the subject. It is therefore *recommended* that:

1   the Government, trusts and universities make a substantial commitment to further quantitative and qualitative research into the impact of, and best practice in, the provision of early learning in order to test the conclusions of this part of the report, and (where appropriate) to extend or qualify them;

2   those responsible for educational research develop a strategy for clarifying the nature and sequence of child development and 'mastery' learning to provide a theoretical framework for the training and sustaining of professional 'early years' teachers and carers.

3. Lessons from Abroad

'It is in early education where the battle for excellence will be won or lost'

(Ernest Boyer, 1991, *Ready to Learn*)

> This chapter considers what can be learned from the experience and practice of other countries. It reveals that investment in effective early learning can provide significant social and economic returns for both developing and developed countries. But the needs of children and parents, and the demands of the labour market, must be considered together. Nations where compulsory state education begins at the age of six (or even seven) are readier to recognise the importance of early learning, and to make provision for it, than those countries where it begins at five. There has been a recent rapid expansion of pre-school education throughout the world, and this process seems likely to continue. Britain, with Ireland and the Netherlands, is out of step with developments in the rest of Europe. The main features of good practice in the management of pre-school education are set out. There is a recommendation for keeping the changing international situation under review.

Introduction

3.1   Not only in the UK, but also in many other countries, there is a growing recognition of the importance of early learning and pre-school education. Lifelong learning and learning for life and work need to start in infancy. Throughout the developed world – and also in some developing nations like India and Brazil – there has been rapid and substantial growth in pre-school education during the last 30 years. This change is undoubtedly linked to the changing pattern of employment in which unskilled work (itself a contradiction in terms) is gradually fading away. Modern jobs require continued learning. Modern societies are learning societies in which knowledge is power. But this growth has also been associated with, and in part caused by, the increasing number of women in the work-force. It is estimated that almost half of the women in Great Britain with children under the age of five will be in employment by 2001 (see appendix G). Where economic pressures drive both parents into paid employment, and equity requires that neither should be prevented from working, three things tend to happen: the introduction of paid parental leave, the recognition of some public responsibility for the care of children of employed parents, and the public provision of nursery education for children from the age of three. Denmark has travelled furthest along this road: with over 90% of women with children in the labour force, it provides a high standard of publicly-funded services for children and their parents. Other nations are following. All are seeking the best way of reconciling and responding to the needs of the labour market, parents and children. Perhaps the first lesson from abroad is that none of these needs can be met in isolation: they must be considered together.

3.2   The main focus of this report is upon young children and the importance of early learning. Like slaves and women in earlier times, children have no vote. And so their interests are liable to be neglected. The United Nations Children's Fund (UNICEF) estimates that some

$25 billion per year are required 'to bring to an end the age-old evils of child malnutrition, preventable disease and widespread illiteracy'. This sum could purchase two or three Channel Tunnels, or one new airport for Hong Kong, or half the cigarettes smoked in Europe each year. So there can be no excuse. Failure to defeat these avoidable evils in the future will have to be explained, not in terms of possibilities, but of priorities. And much has already been achieved. Since the end of the Second World War infant mortality rates have halved, average life expectancy has increased by a third, and in the developing world the proportion of children starting school has risen to over three quarters. There is a new hope – and a new urgency. The World Summit for Children, held at the United Nations in 1990, adopted a range of goals for the year 2000: these included 'basic education for all children and completion of primary education by at least 80%' and 'a halving of the adult illiteracy rate and the achievement of equal educational opportunities for males and females'. Most nations have now agreed to adopt the United Nations *Convention on the Rights of the Child* and work towards these goals. UNICEF's report on *The State of the World's Children 1993* shows how they can be achieved.

3.3   A young child, puzzled by the formal language of the *Convention on the Rights of the Child*, and seeking to grasp its meaning for children, asked: 'shall they all read?'. She asked the right question. Literacy is the key to personal, social and national development. The Save the Children Fund has shown how the achievement of literacy by children (and parents) is the first step towards economic development. The chain of cause and effect works like this. Those who can read, learn to observe elementary rules of health care. This in turn enables parents to gain confidence in the survival of children into adult life. Without this confidence, parents are unlikely to limit the size of their families. And so the control of populations becomes impossible. Development is defeated by uncontrolled growth of populations. UNICEF seeks $25 billion per year to control the major childhood diseases, halve child malnutrition, reduce child deaths by four million a year, bring safe water and sanitation to all communities, make family planning universally available, and provide a basic education for all children. The attainment of the last of these objectives (basic education) by itself will enable poor communities to make substantial progress towards the remaining goals. The second lesson from abroad is that investment in effective early learning can provide significant social and economic returns for both developing and developed countries.

Patterns of provision

3.4   Most compulsory state elementary schooling in Europe starts at the age of six, or even in a few countries seven, and this is also true for much of the rest of the world (e.g. Japan six, USA six to eight). Table 1 (opposite) sets out some relevant comparative figures. A fuller account of the position is given in appendix F. In France, pre-primary schools (*écoles maternelles*), catering for two- to five-year-olds were started a century ago, and now serve over 95% of children aged three to five (inclusive). Although attendance is voluntary, local authorities are required by law to provide pre-primary education except in the smallest communes. The education given is intended to develop children's personalities and prepare them for elementary school. France has recently set itself targets for further extending pre-school education.

3.5   In Italy, pre-school education is provided in both public and private nursery schools and, while attendance is optional, 90% of children age three to five (inclusive) attend full-time,

Table 1. International comparisons of compulsory school age and % of children attending publicly funded services.

	Compulsory school age	% of children attending publicly funded services aged (years):			
		3	4	5	3-5
Belgium (1991)	6	97	99	98	98
Denmark (1992)	7	76	81	79	79
Finland (1992)	7	44	49	53	60
France (1991)	6	98	101	99	99
Germany (1990)	6	-	-	-	77
Greece (1991)	5.5	-	-	CS	88(*)
Ireland (1991)	6	1(+)	55(+)	98	51(+*)
Italy (1992)	6	-	-	-	91
Luxembourg (1990)	5	7	95	CS	67(*)
Netherlands (1991)	5	(+)	98	CS	67(*)
Norway (1992)	7	49	60	68	53
Portugal (1991)	6	28	44	63	45
Spain (1991)	6	28	94	100	74
Sweden (1992)	7	63	67	75	68
Britain (1991)	5	41(+)	58(+)	CS	65(+*)

CS *indicates where 5-year-olds are covered wholly or partly by compulsory schooling (and in these cases, a 100% attendance level for 5-year-olds is included in the '3-5' column);*
+ *indicates that a source of publicly-funded provision is not included, because data is not available;*
* *indicates that a substantial qualification exists concerning the statistic for the whole 3-5 age range.*

six days a week. The objectives are to reinforce the influence and efforts of the family and to prepare for primary schooling. Although nursery schools have no formal curriculum, educational guidelines have been laid down. The Montessori method, which was originally developed for disadvantaged children in Rome, is often used in the private sector, but in general the system has a more teacher-centred and structured style than in other developed countries. In some parts of Italy, childcare programmes are also available from infancy and seen as an accepted part of community life.

3.6   There are three kinds of pre-primary schooling in Germany: the kindergarten caters for children aged three to five (inclusive); in some Länder primary schools have reception classes (*Vorklassen*) for five-year-olds; and school kindergartens admit children of compulsory school age who are too immature for primary education. Kindergartens are mainly within the remit of the Ministry of Health, Family, Youth and Social Affairs, although four-fifths of the funding is from private sources, including the Church. Nominal fees are payable, in practice only by those who can afford them. Staff include teachers, social education workers and children's nurses. Pre-primary education is based on the principle of 'purposeful play' and does not attempt to start the '3 Rs' or the equivalent of 'Key Stage 1'. Reunification of Germany has provided an impetus to raise provision in the former West Germany to the level of what was available in East Germany. At present, nearly 80% of children are in preschool programmes. A target has been set to give every child aged three to five the right to a place at a kindergarten by the beginning of 1996.

3.7   In the USA, rather over half of children aged three to six (inclusive) take part in some kind of peer group activity – either part-time in kindergarten (often associated with a local school), or in a nursery school (often privately run) or in parent co-operatives (employing and assisting a qualified teacher). Community daycare centres offer full-time care for the children of working mothers or whose parents are ill, and the modest fees are supplemented with charitable and government funds. Child development centres cater for those living in disadvantaged areas, mainly under the 'Head Start' programme, with state and federal support. Two years ago, President Bush summoned all the state governors to an educational summit meeting to set out goals for the year 2000. The first goal was that all children should come to school 'ready to learn'. This goal was inspired by a report entitled *Ready to Learn: a mandate for the nation* written by Ernest L Boyer, president of the Carnegie Foundation for the Advancement of Teaching and a distinguished former US Education Secretary. He called for spending on the 'Head Start' programme to be increased from two to eight billion dollars by 1995, describing this as 'an investment that would pay off handsomely in the long run'. The new administration has responded: 'Head Start' funding is to be increased by 46% to over $4 billion this year.

3.8   New Zealand, stimulated by the findings of the High/Scope programmes, undertook a major review of childhood services, which was published in 1988. *Education to be More* is a model of its kind, and one of the inspirations of this report. It went back to first principles, asking: what sort of services have we got? what do we need? how can we meet the needs of children? The report set out the cost and benefits of early childhood care and education for the various relevant groups. It concluded: 'The benefits of complementary early childhood care and education are proven without doubt by research and by experience. Parents know the difference it makes to their children and what a support it can be for themselves. Any principal or junior class teacher will comment on the difference early care and education experience makes to children's ability to learn. Children who enter school without the skills of their peers are likely to be disadvantaged. They start school with a high risk of failure – an important consideration when unskilled employment is disappearing. Early childhood care and education can bridge the skills and knowledge gap, before such children slide into a downward spiral.' (Meade, 1988) The Labour Government accepted the report and set reform in motion with a policy document *Before Five*, in which the Education Minister affirmed that 'improvements in this sector are an investment in the future'. The new policy left the existing diverse system (not unlike that in the UK) in place, put a reorganised Ministry of Education in charge and set up an Early Childhood Development Unit to provide co-ordination, support and training. The new early childhood sector was to have equal status with other sectors of education, its own block grant, and graded increases of funding over four years.

3.9   When the National Government replaced Labour shortly afterwards, there were fears that the new policy would be abandoned. It had been brought in 'despite a declining economy, apathy amongst politicians, and resistance from the Treasury', as one expert observed. But, although there have been some cuts, the integrated system of care and education remains intact. New Zealand has decided to maintain a diversity of services – not unlike the pattern of provision in the UK – but to make funding dependent on their achieving nationally-determined standards. The new Minister pointed out that although participation in early childhood education has doubled since 1980, New Zealand spends only 4.1% of its total education budget on that sector, compared with 28.1% on higher education. He asked why that should be so, when reliable research showed that early childhood education gives students and the tax-payer the best return on investment. His own answers to that question have a resonance in the UK: early childhood is seen as a woman's issue; there are divisions within and between the educational and care services; proposals for policy changes in higher education are met by effective lobbying and demonstrations – pre-school children cannot vote, lobby or march. Nonetheless, the Minister reaffirmed that his government saw early childhood education as an economic imperative as well as a social responsibility. In an impressive discussion document *Education for the 21st Century* (1993) the New Zealand Government proposed a range of ambitious targets – including the aim of providing early childhood education programmes for 95% of three- and four-year-olds by 2001.

3.10   What is clear from even as abbreviated a survey as this is the variety in patterns of provision for pre-school education. Table 1 sets out the situation in the European Union (see also appendix F of this report). While it is true that 'what is needed, and what remains lacking in all member states is a comprehensive and coherent programme for reconciling childcare, employment and equality of opportunity' (Moss, 1990, *Childcare in the European Communities 1985-1990*), it is also true that there is growing interest in these issues, their priority is being recognised and significant changes are occurring in many countries. While Denmark stands out as the leader in Europe, Ireland, the Netherlands and the UK are the laggards. These countries make little or no provision for nursery education, instead using playgroups and early entry to primary schools as substitutes. The Netherlands has recently lowered the age at which children start school from six to five; in the UK (though to a lesser extent in Scotland) there has been a similar *de facto* lowering from age five to four-plus. Neither of these strategies is necessarily wrong, *provided* systematic opportunities for high-quality early learning are thereby made available. Unfortunately children attend playgroups on average for only five to six hours a week, and early entry to primary school tends to lead to the premature introduction of the formal curriculum (Key Stage 1) and inappropriate adult:child ratios. The substitutes are not working. In some the level of staff training is variable, and in others the curriculum is inappropriate. It is the contention of this report that the UK is out of step with what is established or emergent good practice elsewhere in Europe – and beyond. The third lesson from abroad is that Britain is not only on the wrong track, but dangerously ignorant (or complacent) about its situation.

3.11   Moss summarised the contrast between Britain and the rest of Europe as follows: 'This brief overview highlights a number of broad and widespread features of early childhood services in the European Community, including the introduction of parental leave, a recognition of some public responsibility for the children of employed parents (though in most cases, with a large shortfall in the supply of publicly funded services), and a recognition of the need to develop nursery education as a generally available service for children over three (and here, the shortfall in supply is generally far less). In all three respects, Britain differs: no parental leave; an explicit rejection of any public responsibility to support working parents and their children; and an earlier acceptance of the principle of nursery education, in the 1972 White Paper, subsequently abandoned. The situation in Britain has been strongly influenced by the view that care and education of young children is mainly a private matter (the main exception being where child, parent or family are deemed to have some inadequacy or disability). The approach in mainland Europe has been more influenced by concepts of social solidarity, emphasising the importance of providing support to adults in the parenting phase of their life course, which is recognised to be (like childhood) of wider social significance.' (Moss, 1992, in Pugh G., (Ed.). *Contemporary Issues in the Early Years*, p.35)

Integrated models

3.12   While in the past some countries (e.g. the USA) have made very clear distinctions between the functions of care and education, this is now changing. Care and education should be integrated. Competent childcare inevitably requires attention to learning. Education embraces care. Good teachers both care for, and care about, the children in their charge. Similarly, good parents understand that caring for a child involves the encouragement of early learning. The 'seamless web' linking education and care is a key feature of best practice. This principle has some important consequences for the organisation, responsibility and training of staff for early learning, and its links with the home (on the one hand) and the primary school (on the other).

3.13   Bruner, 1980, *Under Fives in Britain* argues that 'the full-time care of children at home in the early years preceding school is neither desirable for many families nor, given that fact, is it good for children. Indeed, it can now be taken as certain that an opportunity to be away from home in a pre-school helps the child to develop socially, intellectually and emotionally'. Recognition of this has led a number of nations to make provision not only for pre-school education between three and the start of primary schooling, but also to integrate this organised early learning into provision for extended daycare – and to move towards systematic provision for children under the age of three. Denmark leads the way. There primary education begins at seven. Some 85% of children of three to six (inclusive) attend some form of publicly-funded service. Most go to kindergartens offering full-time provision, with nearly all six-year-olds attending part-time pre-school classes at primary schools. 'The main distinguishing feature of Denmark, however, is the high level of publicly funded services for children under three. These services (either group care or organised childminding, though it is also possible for a small group of parents to combine to employ a shared nanny and claim public funds) provide for nearly half of all under threes, and Denmark is the only EC country where publicly funded provision accounts for most of the children in this age group who attend some form of early childhood service' (Moss, 1992, in Pugh G., (Ed.). *Contemporary Issues in the Early Years*, p.34-5). The Danish model, providing an integrated response to the demands of the labour market, and the needs of both children and parents, is an impressive example of what in all probability is the shape of things to come in the developed world. One of the most interesting and significant features of childhood services in Denmark is the increasing role being played by men. By and large, in the rest of the world (including the UK) these services are staffed by women, with the inevitable but regrettable consequences of the lack of male 'caring' models and low status for the service.

3.14   While education and care are rarely seen as separate needs today, many countries still have somewhat different ministerial portfolios or departmental responsibilities for the two aspects of 'edu-care'. But this, too, is increasingly changing. Many nations (and governments) have come to view the period of early years care and education as a whole. Recent changes in countries as diverse as France, Hungary and Poland, Canada and the USA, all demonstrate this feature. For example, since 1988 education and care for children from the age of two-and-a-half have been integrated within the educational brief in British Columbia and Alberta. In France the *écoles maternelles*, established under separate governance since 1871, now form part of the general ministerial responsibility for education. In Spain, a new law has brought together nursery education and childcare services; already some 70% of children aged three to five (inclusive) attend full-time nursery education. And similar changes are planned in several of the states of Australia. An integrated model of organisation for early learning and daycare requires an integration of responsibility for the service.

3.15 The integration of early education and care has consequences for the training of staff. This does not mean that all staff are (or should be) trained in the same way. Only in the UK is the issue polarised in the fatuous public debate about the relative merits of professional 'early years' teachers versus 'mums' army'. We need both – and both need appropriate training. Increasingly, pre-school teachers are being trained alongside primary teachers (or on courses of similar length, complexity and status) in other countries. Furthermore, support-staff (nursery nurses and assistants) are themselves receiving thorough training (often at university diploma level) in many nations. After the age of eighteen, the normal length of early years teacher training is four years – though some five-year courses exist in Australia, Canada, Malta and the USA. Britain and (parts of) Germany stand apart in devoting substantial portions of teacher training to school-based practice. Such an approach to training needs to beware of diminishing – or denying the importance of – the theory of the development of learning in children. Britain seems to have the largest number of diverse and confused routes to qualified teacher status, but (unlike many countries) fails to provide a clear and open route for support staff (nursery nurses and aides) to progress to the status of trained early years teacher. Recent development of NVQs/SVQs has offered the promise of improved and more accessible training. In Scotland, the redesign of college-based courses by SCOTVEC (Scottish Vocational Education Council) is particularly encouraging.

3.16 There is inevitably considerable variation in the (trained) adult:child ratio throughout the world. On the whole the provision of adults is more generous in pre-school than in primary schools. If High/Scope is increasingly being recognised as an example of 'good practice', it is noteworthy that the ratios are almost identical to the RSA 'rule of thumb' which suggests that (throughout the educational system) the appropriate provision is one (trained) adult to the number of children (or students) equivalent to double their average age (i.e. 'class sizes' of 6 for three-year-olds, 12 for six-year-olds, 24 for twelve-year-olds, and so on). The intention and effect of such a rule is to tilt resources back towards early learning – without making substantial new demands on educational budgets.

3.17 The integration of care and education should not mean the imposition of an 'academic' curriculum on three-year-olds. Instead, there is a widespread acceptance that the diverse, informally-assessed practice which derives from the principles of active learning and 'purposeful play' should spread upwards, like a beneficial infection, into primary schooling. By such means it is hoped to achieve a smooth linkage (or 'articulation') between the pre-school and primary stages. However, it is never easy to provide for problem-free progression (in content or process of learning) from one stage of education to the next. Joint – or integrated – staff training would help. As with the link between home and pre-school, it is easier to see what is needed than to deliver it.

Conclusions

3.18 This summary review of the patterns of provision and integrated models for early learning in other countries (more fully set out in appendix F) leads to the following *conclusions*:

a) investment in effective early learning can provide significant social and economic returns for both developing and developed countries;

b) the needs of children and parents, and the demands of the labour market, should be considered together;

c) paradoxically, nations where compulsory state education begins at the age of six (or even seven) are readier to recognise the importance of early learning, and make provision for it, than those countries where it begins at the age of five;

d) throughout the world – especially in developed countries, and most notably in Europe – there has been a rapid expansion in pre-school education during the last 30 years: this process appears set to continue;

e) Britain, together with Ireland and the Netherlands, is out of step with developments in the remainder of the European Union;

f) the salient features of good practice in the direction and management of the provision of early learning appear to include:

    i.   the integration of education and care

    ii. unified responsibility for provision

    iii. targets for growth by a specified year

    iv. coherent and thorough training of early years teachers and support staff

    v. a curriculum based on the principle of 'purposeful play'

    vi. effective linkage between the home and pre-school, and smooth progression between pre-school and primary school

    vii. adequate resources.

3.19   While these conclusions are secure in the light of what is known currently, there is considerable change in train or impending in a number of countries. The principles, policies and practice of early learning and pre-school education are all under review in many different places. Accordingly it is *recommended* that:

3   **the RSA should plan and organise a major international conference on 'good practice in pre-school education' to review and update the findings of this report in 1995.**

4. Patterns of Provision in the UK

'The status quo is merely one of the options: be aware of others'

(The 13th touchstone for a learning organisation)

This chapter reviews the patterns of provision in the UK. It identifies seven major types, considers the case of children with special educational needs, and recognises combined Nursery Centres as a model close to the ideal. But the existing diverse pattern of provision lacks coherence, co-ordination or direction. It fails to meet the needs of either children or parents. It is unevenly and inequitably distributed. It does not provide an assurance of high quality. Many of those most in need – and most likely to benefit – miss out. The quantitative statistical base and the qualitative knowledge base are inadequate and incomplete. Governments have failed over many years to establish a national framework within which local developments could take place. While funding appears to be the major impediment to progress, in reality the problem is one of priorities. Pre-school education should be among a nation's first priorities. There is a strong recommendation for a Government review and action.

Introduction

4.1   Diversity is the hallmark of pre-school provision for the under-fives in the UK. But not choice. Or coherence. There is a wide range of provision, including nursery schools, nursery classes, nursery units in primary schools, day nurseries and, of course, pre-school playgroups. But neither market mechanisms nor planned public provision are enabling parents to find the pre-school education and care they want for their children, or children to make the right start to learning and life. Both the following statements (one defensive, the other critical, of the *status quo*) are true: 'linking all types of provision together, over 90% of three- and four-year-olds now attend some form of education or other group provision'; 'the UK as a whole is near the bottom of the league for publicly-funded pre-school educational places'. How can that be?

4.2   The previous chapter showed that, in contrast with emerging good practice in Europe, the UK seems to use two strategies as *substitutes* for high-quality nursery education – early entry to primary schools, and playgroups. The importance of these two strategies is clear from statistics for the percentage and numbers of children attending different types of provision in England in 1992 recently quoted by a Minister:

	'Local Authority nursery schools	*Nursery classes* (at primary schools)	*Reception classes* (at primary schools)	*Pre-School playgroups*	*Independent schools*
%	4	22	23	41	4
'000s	52	278	300	525	46

(The percentages total 94 because some children attend more than one type of provision.)'

This is an unsatisfactory, and potentially misleading, statement of the position. There are other ways of presenting the general picture, for example:

* over 45% of places in pre-school provision depend on parental fees, rather than public provision (60%)⁺
* over 40% of children attend playgroups on average for two sessions (less than 10 hours) per week (nearly 60%)⁺
* over 75% of children are being admitted to primary schools before their fifth birthday
* Local Education Authority provision of nursery education caters for a range from 0 - 80%+ of three- and four-year-olds in different localities.

(⁺ *The figures in brackets include children under the age of three.*)

Table 2 shows the number of places in most types of early childhood provision in 1980 and 1991. It demonstrates the conflicting slow growth of publicly-funded services and rapid expansion of the private sector (childminders and private day nurseries).

Table 2.   *Number of places in early childhood care and education provision, 1980, 1991, England.*
Source: Sylva K. and Moss P., November 1992 (32)

Types of provision	1980	1991	% change 1980-1991
Nursery education	130,997	177,863	+36
Reception class	205,673	272,178	+32
Local authority day nurseries	28,437	27,039	-5
Private nurseries	22,017	79,029	+259
Playgroups	367,868	428,420	+16
Childminders	98,495	233,258	+137

Table 3 (see pp.34-35) gives a more detailed breakdown of the various *types* of provision. See NCB Table for breakdown on England, Wales and Scotland★. However, it is important to state a general caution against uncritical reliance on the statistics quoted in this and other reports. Peter Moss's authoritative appendix F to this report sets out the problem (and the position) as clearly as possible.

4.3   Nonetheless, it is clear from these figures that 'early childhood care and education services are unevenly distributed, and receive limited public funding; most provision is in the private market and depends on parents' ability to pay. The UK has one of the lowest levels of publicly-funded pre-school services in Europe', (Sylva and Moss, 1992, *Learning Before School*). Furthermore, the available provision fails in a number of ways to satisfy the over-riding requirement for good early childhood services, namely high quality. Nursery education and local authority day nurseries run the risk of creating the ghetto effect (2.15) because of scarcity and rationing of places. The reception classes in primary schools run the risk of imposing an inappropriate curriculum with insufficient and non-specialist staff. Playgroups run the risk of providing too brief a period of attendance, with inadequate equipment and inadequately-trained staff. The private sector is unlikely to serve the children from disadvantaged backgrounds, where the potential for benefit is greatest. Others have characterised the pattern of provision in the UK as lacking commitment, co-ordination and cash. In earlier times, it would have been called a public scandal.

★ National Children's Bureau, 1991, Statistics: Under Fives and Pre-School Services

Types of provision

4.4   There are seven major types of provision (apart from parents at home), and several minor types. The first is **nursery education**, which is designed to further children's emotional, social, physical and cognitive development, complementing the learning that takes place in the home. Nursery schools and nursery classes run by Local Education Authorities provide free education for children between the ages of two-and-a-half and five. They are staffed by specially trained teachers and nursery nurses. (Trained) adult:child ratios stand at about 1:13. Availability of places varies significantly by locality, ranging from 0% to 80%+ of three- and four-year-olds. About four-fifths of enrolled children attend part-time, usually for five half-days a week. Nursery education provides for about a quarter of three- and four-year-old children (about 4% in nursery schools and some 21% in nursery classes).

4.5   **Reception classes** in primary schools admit just over three-quarters of children at age four, although children are not obliged to start school until the term after their fifth birthday. Policies on early admission vary between Local Education Authorities. In the past, it has been usual for children to be admitted at the start of the term in which they will become five: these children are known as 'rising fives'. But the trend towards once-yearly admission has led to some younger four-year-olds being admitted to reception classes. This form of 'pre-school' education is free. Its quality varies widely, depending on a range of factors including the nature of the curriculum, the provision of staffing (which is rarely as favourable as in nursery education), and the training of staff. Primary schools employ trained teachers, few of whom have received specialised nursery training; and some also employ nursery nurses and (untrained) support staff. The children attend full-time.

4.6   **Local Authority day nurseries** provide full-time or part-time care for children who are deemed to need specialist help. They are run by social services departments. Day nurseries are tending to move away from simply providing care for 'problem children' towards an approach involving work with parents and children together. These 'family centres' can offer, not only counselling and classes for the parents, but also in many cases nursery education for the children. Places are allocated according to a system of priorities. The age range catered for is from birth to four (inclusive), but normally day nurseries do not admit children younger than one-and-a-half. The staff are trained nursery nurses, sometimes with additional qualifications in social work. Where there is a nursery class, it is normal for a trained teacher to be employed (or seconded). Day nurseries make only a small contribution to early learning and the care of pre-school children: they cater for less than 1% of under fives.

4.7   **Private and Voluntary day nurseries** are similar to Local Authority nurseries. But they also include a variety of rather different kinds of provision: community nurseries, all-day playgroups, workplace nurseries, partnership nurseries and all-day crèches. They must be registered and inspected by local authority social services departments. They provide full or sessional care for children of parents who can afford the fees. The provision is required to satisfy national standards laid down in the Children Act 1989. Training is variable: no minimum standard is required in this respect. The recent growth in workplace nurseries is particularly important and interesting. It is bound to raise the question whether young children are best served by nurseries close to their home, or close to their parent's place of work. If both patterns continue to develop, it is not clear how systematic provision for all children can be satisfactorily organised or managed. This is a very rapidly growing sector and currently provides for about 2½% of under fives.

Table 3.   Statistics: Day care and pre-school education 1991. Provisions and costs in Great Britain.

Type of Provision	% of children	Hours	Ages	Approximate cost to parents
Day care	**% of 0-4**			
Childminders	7%	All day	0-4	£1.50 per hour £50 per week
Local Authority day nurseries/family centres	1%	Some all day, some sessional	0-4 (but few under 2)	Means tested
Private day nurseries, partnership and workplace nurseries	2.5%	All day	0-4	Between £45 - £150 per week depending on age of child and availability of subsidy
Education and Play	**% of 3-4**			
LEA nursery schools and classes	26%	Termtime: usually 2½ hours a day	3-4	Free
Infant classes	21%	Termtime: 9am - 3.30pm	mainly 4	Free
Playgroups	60% (1.8 children per place)	Usually 2½ hours for 2/3 days a week, some all day	2½ - 4	£1.70 per 2½ hour session
Private nursery and other schools	3.5%	Usually 9am - 3.30pm	2½ - 4	Various fees
Services on which there are no national statistics				
Combined nursery centres	about 50 centres	All day	0-4	Education free, day care means tested
Family centres (May include some LA day nurseries)	about 500 members of Family Centre Network (Dec.93)	Usually all day	Vary	Vary
Out of school/holiday clubs	700 clubs (Dec.93)	before and after school, holidays	Vary	Vary

% do not add up to 100 because some children attend two types of provision.

Provided by	Staffing	Training	Ratios
Private arrangement	Registered childminders	Variable. No national requirements	1:3 0-5 1:6 5-7
Local Authority Social Services	Mainly nursery nurses	NNEB/DPQS/BTec SNNB/SCOTVEC Units	1:3 0-2 1:4 2-3 1:8 3-5
Employers, private organisations and individuals	Nursery nurses, some untrained staff	at least half staff must be trained - as above	1:3 0-2 1:4 2-3 1:8 3-4
Local Authority Education	Nursery teachers nursery nurses	Degree and PGCE/ BEd NNEB	1 (teacher):23 1 (all staff):10/13
Local Authority Education	Primary teachers teaching assistant or nursery nurse recommended	Degree and PGCE/ BEd NNEB SNNB/SCOTVEC Units	1:30/40 (better if nursery nurse employed)
Parents and voluntary groups	Playgroup leader	Foundation course/ diploma in playgroups practice	1:8 3-5
Private individuals and organisations	Not specified: often teacher or NNEB	Unknown	1:8 3-4 1:20/30 5+
Local authority education and social services, sometime health and voluntary sector input	Nursery teachers, nursery nurses	as for nursery schools/classes and day nurseries	as for nursery schools/classes and day nurseries
Local Authority social services, health authorities, voluntary sector	nursery nurses, social workers, range of staff	Varied	Depends on nature of centre
Schools, leisure depts, voluntary sector	playleaders, community workers, volunteers	Unknown	1:8 5-7

Devised by Early Childhood Unit National Children's Bureau, drawing on government statistics and information from voluntary organisations.

4.8   **Private nursery schools** are open for the length of the normal school day. Little information is available, since (if they take only children under the age of five) they are not obliged to register as schools with the Department for Education; but they are required to register with local authority social services departments. There are no figures available on the number of such schools or their staffing or the fees charged. About 3½% of children aged three to four are attending private nursery schools. This is also an expanding sector.

4.9   **Playgroups** cater for children aged three (sometimes two-and-a-half) to four (inclusive), aiming to provide education through play. Parents pay a fee for each session. Groups offer support to parents, and many provide opportunities for learning and involvement. Local availability varies: numbers appear to be highest where Local Education Authority nursery education is most scarce. The playgroup movement gives emphasis to the principle that parents are the prime educators of their children. There are many different kinds of playgroups, but two-thirds are community groups – managed by parent committees and run by playgroup workers with parent helpers. In England group leaders are usually trained through the Pre-School Playgroups Association (PPA), a registered educational charity to which most playgroups belong. Scotland, Wales, and Northern Ireland make different arrangements. Some playgroups are run by local authorities or private individuals. Almost two-thirds are non-profit making groups run by committees of parents; about a third are run by individuals (either on a commercial or non-profit making basis); and some 3% are run by local authority social services departments. Most children attend playgroups for two or three half-day sessions a week. Although most groups remain open for five sessions a week, they have to ration attendance to accommodate more children. An increasing number of groups operate extended hours. Most playgroups include children with special needs, but 'opportunity playgroups' cater specifically for them (alongside other children) and provide links with specialist medical or psychological expertise. Playgroups are required to register with the local authority social services department and are regularly inspected to ensure they conform to national standards. Roughly half of all children aged three and four attend playgroups: estimates vary from 41% (proportion quoted by a Government Minister in the Department for Education) to 60% (estimate published by the National Children's Bureau).

4.10   **Childminders**, who must be registered with local authority social services departments, take children under the age of five into their homes for two or more hours per day, for which the parents pay a fee. The arrangement is usually a private one between parent and minder, though some local authorities sponsor the placement of 'priority' children with 'Day Carers' or 'Day Foster Parents'. Although about half of registered childminders are members of the National Childminding Association, not a lot is known in detail about this sector. Whether it makes a substantial contribution to early learning (as opposed to care) is doubtful. There are wide variations in the hours worked, facilities provided, and the training of childminders. Recommended ratios are 1:3 for children under five; this includes the childminder's own children (if any). These ratios tend to be enforced as a condition of registration. This sector is growing rapidly and currently provides places for about 7% of under fives.

4.11   These seven types of provision, do not, however, give the full picture. There are also some minor categories which do not demand detailed discussion here – except for the **Combined Nursery Centres** which offer an excellent model for future provision by fully integrating care and education. Although no two are precisely the same, combined nursery centres offer a flexible combination of daycare and nursery education. In addition to this desirable integration of care and early learning, they often offer support and facilities for parents on a 'drop-in' basis, a centre for toy libraries and help for families with special needs. Some go further and provide adult education and child health advice in addition. Of all existing types of provision, combined nursery centres come closest to the ideal which this report seeks to promote.

4.12 Children with special educational needs may be provided for in any of the above settings and will also be amongst the estimated 10% of children at home in the care of parents or nannies (see 4.13). Some of the young children whose difficulties or disabilities are most pronounced and have been identified at an early stage, receive additional support from a wide range of medical, educational and social services. Nationally, at least 4,000 children receive support from Portage projects (Kiernan, 1993). Portage is a scheme which provides support to the development of the child by working alongside parents. Some children with special educational needs are placed in special daycare provision. This may be attached to a child development centre or other NHS provision where there is ready access to medical, para-medical services and in some centres a range of further support services. Whether or not they have a statement under the 1981 Education Act (or in future under the 1993 Education Act) children with special educational needs may be given priority admission, or early admission to nursery education. However, where there is not widespread provision this may lead to over-concentrations of children with a range of difficulties. The special educational needs of many more children are not identified or may not emerge until they start in educational provision. The importance of good quality early learning provision for these children is obvious: without it they are less likely to be identified and given appropriate help as soon as possible. The Warnock Report advised: 'While recognising the financial constraints, we would like to see a considerable expansion of opportunities for nursery education for young children with special needs on a part-time as well as a full-time basis. We do not, however, believe that it would at present be either practicable or desirable to seek to achieve this through a policy of positive discrimination in the admission of children to nursery schools and classes. Rather, we recommend that the provision for nursery education for all children should be substantially increased as soon as possible, since this would have the consequence that opportunities for nursery education for young children with special needs could be correspondingly extended' (Warnock Report, 5.51, 1978).

4.13 Finally a considerable group of young children remain at home in the care of parents or nannies – or are placed with unregistered childminders – up to the age of five. This group appears to contain some 10% of children aged three to four. Readers might be forgiven if they feel confused at this point. The complexity of the pattern of provision in the UK, the confusion of the statistics and the absence of principled direction of the early childhood care and education services are obvious. It is a service characterised by diversity: diversity in the types of provision, diversity within each type, and diversity of quality overall. The following table is designed to simplify the picture – though readers should recall G K Chesterton's comment that 'he who simplifies, simply lies'. It seeks to reveal the following critical distinctions: on the vertical dimension, the age of children (0-2, 3-4, and 0-4 combined); on the horizontal dimension, first, the distinction between centre-based provision and (entirely) home-based provision – second, the distinction between private and public provision – and third, the distinction between 'education' (provided by the Local Authority) and 'care' (provided by Social Services). (Of course, it fails to reveal the critical distinction between high- and low-quality provision, or the relative amount of time spent in different kinds of provision.)

| | Centre-based provision | | | | Nursery | No Centre-based provision | |
| | Public | | Private | | | Childminders | Homecare |
	Education (pre-school)	Social Services	Playgroups	Crèche/ Children's Centres			
children aged 0 – 2	none	nb	na	nb	none	nb	na
3 – 4	26%	nb	60%	nb	3.5%	nb	na
0 – 4*	26%	1%	60%	2.5%	3.5%	7%	na

nb – not broken down   na – not available

* the percentages add up to 100% (without any figures for those children cared for totally at home) because children may attend more than one type of provision. No statistics are available for children at home.

Commentary

4.14   The first thing that needs to be said about the survey presented in the preceding paragraphs is that the statistical base is inadequate and the information incomplete, uncertain and (in places) conflicting. The Rumbold Report found the same difficulty. Its words remain apt today: 'The data we are able to give suffer from a number of defects. The Department (for Education) and the Department of Health collect figures at different times in the year and on different bases, educational figures being for children and childcare figures being for places. The figures are not complete: those for family centres and combined nursery places do not appear, nor those for peripatetic nursery teachers. For these reasons it is not possible to derive a comprehensive statistical base. The national statistics for particular services may conceal wide local variations in what is available. Where they permit meaningful comparisons to be drawn these relate entirely to the quantity of the facilities provided and say nothing of their quality. We believe a more satisfactory statistical base is needed as a basis for policy making and recommend that the two Departments commission a study to establish how this might be done.' (*Starting with Quality*, 1990.) This recommendation fell upon stony ground. Nothing has been done. Although all Local Authorities were required to review their services in 1992 (under provisions of the Children Act 1989), the results have not yet been collected, aggregated and published on a national basis.

4.15   There might be a variety of reasons for this neglect. One is the lack of real responsibility and the division of (national) responsibility between the two departments of state. This division in part arises from, and in part reinforces, a failure to recognise the principle of the integration of childcare and early learning. But the evidence of research and the lessons from abroad teach the fundamental principle of the 'seamless web' uniting early education and care, 'edu-care'. Those whose primary concern is the health of the child need to understand that good early learning is a critical part of healthy growth; those whose primary concern is education need to understand that 'good teachers should know, but *must care*' (in both senses of 'caring for' and 'caring about'). Education without care doesn't work. This is well understood by most practitioners and many local authorities, but is not reflected in the organisation or behaviour of central government. Successive governments (of different political persuasions) have failed to recognise the need, failed to allocate responsibility, failed to make provision, failed to ensure quality, and failed to collect statistics.

4.16   One particularly glaring consequence of the division of responsibility is the different (sometimes conflicting) requirements for the registration, inspection and standards of provision. The Children Act of 1989 has laid down clear (minimum) national standards and requires local authority social services departments to ensure that they are met. While the Children Act urges co-ordination, the Education Reform Act 1988, and succeeding legislation, makes co-ordination more difficult by reducing the role of Local Education Authorities, and failing to make provision for the definition and maintenance of standards and quality in pre-school education. In its evidence to the House of Commons Select Committee (1989)*, the Association of County Councils stated: 'Educational research has consistently indicated that the most important single step towards the improvement of the quality of education in this country would be to provide a coherent and comprehensive system of pre-school education for all'. This report endorses that statement. And it may be added that, since one of the major requirements for effective early learning is high-quality provision, the Department for Education's lack of interest and (indeed) neglect is little short of disgraceful.

4.17   There are no effective national standards, or advisory norms, for the length of time per week (or the age at which) children should experience centre-based early learning, the training of staff, appropriate ratios of (trained) adults to children**, appropriate resources (buildings and equipment) and indicative costs. This has all been said before, and often, and clearly. The Rumbold Report (1990) *Starting with Quality*, stated: 'we believe that the achievement of greater co-ordination could be greatly helped if central government gave a clear lead, setting a national framework within which local developments could take place'. Why doesn't it happen?

4.18   Margaret Thatcher's 1972 White Paper accepted the principle of nursery education. It has subsequently been abandoned by governments of both left and right. There can be little doubt that the main reason is cost. Ministers have recently estimated that the recurrent cost of 'forcing the state to provide a place for every three- and four-year-old, irrespective of (parental) income' would be over half-a-billion pounds a year, together with 'substantial capital costs'. They challenge those who advocate investment in pre-school education to say where the money would come from, and to state what existing programmes should be cut to provide the necessary resources. While noting that this is a challenge of a kind which others responsible for public provision (the police or the universities, for example) are not required to meet, it is one to which this report offers a response (see Chapter 7): investment in good pre-school education provides a real economic return to society – indeed, the 'payback' of nursery education is clearer and higher than that so far calculated for any other phase of education. At this point, however, it is important to establish that the debate is more about priorities than resources. Developed nations do not discuss whether they can afford what they value highest – clean water, immunisation, disability benefits, national security or the costs of elections and parliament. The importance of early learning is such that it belongs in this list. The European Council of Ministers has urged member states to improve childcare provision; governments may be encouraged to spend 1% of gross domestic product for this purpose (a sum calculated at about £6 billion for the UK by the year 2000). Ministers should consider the words of one of their supporters and himself a recent Minister in the Department for Education: 'Anyone with the money knows that good nursery school-

---

*   Department of Education and Science (1989) *Aspects of Primary Education: the education of children under five*, London: HMI Report.

** There are conflicting recommended ratios: the Children Act requires 1:8 for three- to four-year-olds, while the Education Department advises 1:13 for nursery provision – and permits up to 1:40 in reception classes.

ing is one of the best educational buys available ... The fact that nursery education can give a child a lasting advantage ... is so self-evident that it scarcely needs proof ... How can anyone whose own child has benefited from serious nursery education have the gall to maintain that it is not essential for the children of others?' (George Walden, MP, *Daily Telegraph*, 18 May 1993.)

4.19   When Ministers say the problem is money, they reveal that their priorities are muddled. The statement that over half-a-billion pounds per annum would be required 'to provide a place for every three- and four-year-old', while no doubt intended to discourage the advocates of early learning, confirms and admits that existing patterns of provision are seriously inadequate. It is difficult to accept both that all is well with what we have got, and that so large a sum would be needed to provide what is recognised as 'good practice' elsewhere in the world. In fact, all is not well. Ministers who believe that the diversity of provision in the UK offers a satisfactory service cannot have seriously considered the evidence. Of course, in moving from an unsatisfactory situation to a better one we should use all the resources available – and in particular build on the strengths of both established nursery education and the voluntary pre-school playgroup movement. Ministers who argue that market forces and private provision will respond to the demand and needs for early learning, have not been able to show how the most disadvantaged parents and children will be helped. (Even those parents who are relatively well off are probably experiencing the most difficult economic stage of their lives, as they face the costs of housing and dependent children while managing for a time on one income.) Ministers who are not persuaded that research has yet proved the advantages of pre-school education should consider whether the nation can any longer afford to take the risk of waiting for further confirmation. Bad management is more often characterised by sins of omission, than of commission. Margaret Thatcher saw what was required in 1972. In the intervening 22 years, research and experience abroad have confirmed the wisdom of her acceptance of the principle of nursery education. It is high time to act.

Conclusions

4.20   This brief review of the patterns of provision in the UK suggests the following *conclusions*:
a) the diverse pattern of provision lacks coherence, co-ordination or direction;
b) it fails to meet the needs of either children or parents;
c) it is unevenly and inequitably distributed;
d) it falls short in a number of ways of providing an assurance of high quality, without which the benefits of pre-school education are seriously diminished;
e) many of those most in need, and most likely to benefit, miss out;
f) the quantitative statistical base and the qualitative knowledge base are inadequate and incomplete;
g) the division of responsibility between the Health and Education Departments is a major difficulty;
h) so is the failure to grasp the principle of the integration of childcare and early learning;
i) the Department for Education has neglected its moral responsibilities for supervising, registering, inspecting and ensuring the quality of pre-school education – and has failed to seek and obtain appropriate statutory authority;

j) the Government has failed over many years to establish a national framework within which local developments could take place, building on best practice;

k) while funding appears to be the major impediment to progress, in reality the problem is one of priorities;

l) pre-school education should be among a nation's first priorities;

m) ministers have offered an unconvincing and inadequate defence of the status quo, by setting a high value on diversity (at the expense of quality, effectiveness and choice), by expressing doubt about the value of pre-school education (in the teeth of the evidence of research and the experience of other countries), and by trusting in the private sector (without ensuring either that those most in need – and most likely to benefit – will thereby be provided for or that the provision will be of satisfactory quality).

4.21 Accordingly, it is *recommended* that:

4 parliament, political parties, employers, the media, the churches and other voluntary, community and religious organisations should consider whether the provision for pre-school education in the UK is seriously inadequate, and take steps to persuade the Government to undertake an urgent review and act on its recommendations.

5. The Home and the Community

'It takes a whole village to educate a child'
(African Proverb)

> This chapter considers the role of the home and community. It proposes a strong 'triangle of care' formed by parents, professionals and the community as a whole. The role of parents is the most important. As children's first educators, parents need to be 'warm demanders', to develop confidence and competence in a role which (like any form of demanding work) requires preparation, study and reflection. There should be a real partnership between parents and professionals. The whole community has an interest in, and responsibility for, the welfare and early learning of children. There is an urgent need for (a) introduction of paid parental leave; (b) the provision of care for pre-school children of employed parents; (c) high-quality pre-school education for all children from the age of three. There are four recommendations concerning parenthood; parental education and support; professional training for partnership with parents; and communal responsibility.

Introduction

5.1   All cultures revere pregnancy. A woman with child is recognised as sacred, and normally receives special consideration. She is offered choice food, relieved of heavy work, given a seat on overcrowded buses, entitled to maternity leave, provided with special medical care. (Or so she should be.) Both the community as a whole and a range of professionals rally round to offer support, encouragement and help. And yet none of them can do the job themselves. Only the mother can have the baby. The parent takes precedence. The life-chances of a child depend more on its mother than on any other factor, But, to negotiate the perils of the nine months of pregnancy successfully, a child in the womb needs the loving care of a home, professional experts, and a supportive community. This strong triangle (of parents, professionals and the community) is needed just as much by children after birth as they negotiate the challenges of childhood and adolescence.

5.2   Parents come first. They are both the child's first educators – and the most important influence in the child's life. Their role is fundamental to successful early learning. They stand at the apex of the triangle of support. The High/Scope project has demonstrated that parental involvement is essential to good pre-school education. But neither of the terms 'involvement' or even 'partnership' quite hits the mark. It is as if we were to talk of the mother's *involvement* or *partnership* with the midwife at the birth of the child. It should be the other way round. The primacy of the parental role suggests that parenthood itself needs to be seen as showing some of the characteristics of a skilled occupation, and that parents should approach their role in a 'professional' or 'workmanlike' manner. Parents, as well as children, need to practise 'mastery' learning. If this is so, there will be interesting consequences for the professions at the second point of the triangle – teachers, doctors and social workers, for example. They will need to consider the 'midwifely' or enabling nature of their roles. As for the community as a whole (the third point of the triangle), what responsibility does it have for the education and well-being of its children? and how should such responsibility be discharged? The following sections of this chapter attempt to provide provisional answers to such questions, with the aim of stimulating a wider debate.

Parents

5.3   Parents are the most important people in their children's lives. It is from parents that children learn most, particularly in the early months and years. The critical input of the parents in the child's development and early learning is both self-evident – and yet frequently ignored. Children learn from the moment of birth – if not sooner; their parents and extended family provide both the context in which this learning occurs and the continuity between home, pre-school and school. As children progress into early education or daycare settings their learning continues to be most strongly influenced by the home; the closer the links between parents and nursery, playgroups or childminder, the more effective that learning becomes. Like adults and older children, young children learn best when they are happy and settled, when they are in a familiar and yet stimulating environment, when they receive positive feedback and encouragement which helps develop their emerging sense of identity and self-esteem. Children need 'warm demanders', if they are to thrive. Research suggests that they develop best in highly interactive parent-child relationships, where the adult is consistently responsive to the behaviour initiated by the child, elaborating the child's language and encouraging play, curiosity and exploration. While it is good to answer children's questions, it is even better to encourage them to ask good questions themselves.

5.4   'Modern parenthood is too demanding and complex a task to be performed well merely because we have all once been children' (Kellmer Pringle, 1975). Given the importance of the role of parents as their children's first educators, it is surprising how little attention has been given to the preparation, education and support of parents in this critical task in the UK. While many young adults approach parenthood with confidence and excitement, for others the experience is less positive, more daunting. All parents have skills, but many do not have the confidence to make the best use of them, and few at the outset have all the skills required by modern parenthood. Confidence is vital. Parents can best provide an appropriate context for early learning when they themselves feel confident in their role. Those whose own schooling was unsuccessful or unhappy, or who have no experience of the educational system in the UK, or whose first language is not English, may have difficulty in understanding what is available for their children and lack the confidence to seek help and advice. Even competent, coping parents can find their role diminished and their confidence undermined if they are faced with professional advice which appears unhelpful, condescending or conflicting, or with professionals who always assume that they know best. Conversely, professional support which is open and helpful is enormously encouraging to parents.

5.5   It is a mistake to divide parents into two groups, of sheep and goats: those who are judged to be coping adequately and therefore to need little support; and those who fall below the threshold of adequacy and become the focus for intervention – with the risk of gradually excluding them from responsibility. There can be few parents who do not wish to do all they can to give their children the best start in life; but many who lack the 'permitting circumstances' which could make that a reality. Similarly there can be few parents who are so competent that they can entirely dispense with professional help and community support; but many whose confidence and competence will most surely allow their children to thrive when they are firmly linked into the other two points of the triangle of care. Neither the Swiss Family Robinson, nor the wicked stepmother of fairy stories, are common types of parenthood. Most of us need help to do our best for our children – but not 'disabling help'. (See Pugh and De'Ath, 1989, *Working Towards Partnership in the Early Years*)

5.6   A generation ago it was normal to apply a 'deficit model' to the relationship between parents and professionals. The American Head Start programme, for example, assumed that parents would benefit from the intervention of professionals, organised the relationship on the professionals' terms, and tended to see children as needing to be rescued from inadequate backgrounds. Experience has enabled us to learn better. The Warnock Report (1978) on special educational needs was one of the first official statements to recognise the principle of partnership between parents and professionals; and it is in this area, where parents face particular challenges, that the complementary skills of parents and professionals are most crucial to effective provision. Yet despite some innovative work, practice has often fallen short of the principle. The principle also underpins the Children Act of 1989 and while it has still not fully penetrated professional attitudes, it is best developed in the early childhood services. But even here the issue still tends to be seen in terms of 'parental involvement' – with a hierarchy of levels stretching from *non-participation*, through *support*, *participation* and *partnership*, to *control* – rather than (as here) the formation of a triangle of care, with the parents at the apex. The key question is not how many parents can be persuaded to help in pre-school education, but the quality of the relationship between parents and the professional educators. Real partnership demands a shared sense of purpose, mutual respect, and willingness to negotiate. It requires open, regular and reciprocal communication, where achievements are celebrated, problems confronted, solutions sought and policies implemented *jointly and together*. It takes time and effort and trust. It implies that parental competence is on a par with professional expertise. (See Pugh and De'Ath, 1989, *Working Towards Partnership in the Early Years*) Perhaps this is best recognised in some of the home-teaching schemes, such as Portage, for young children with learning difficulties. The professional works alongside the parent to support the parent's leading role in the educational and social development of the child.

5.7   Research has demonstrated the benefits to children of the active involvement of parents in early childhood education. Indeed, the role of parents was seen in Chapter 2 as one of the five defining features of *high-quality* early education. Parents also benefit, as their confidence in their role and their understanding of it increase. Parental involvement in the early years provides a good foundation for a continuing role for parents as educators throughout the school system. They are able to develop skills as educators through involvement in playgroups and nurseries and in home-visiting projects such as Portage, where they can work with their children alongside trained teachers. The RSA study *Parents in a Learning Society* has identified and initiated a number of projects of this nature. Parents are also starting to contribute to the assessment of their children through the use of profiles and records in nurseries. Here again, the area of special educational needs leads the way. Finally, when parents are managers of pre-school groups, as is the case in community playgroups and nurseries, the partnership between professionals and parents is most evident. Parents benefit from taking responsibility for the playgroup or nursery and from participating in its activities. Apart from developing a better understanding of the needs of young children and of the importance of their own role, many parents go on to enrol in courses which may ultimately lead to a qualification in early childhood care and education. This is particularly important for parents whose own experience of education has been negative. Within parent-run groups, collective action is encouraged and authority shared. For some parents this may be the first opportunity they have had to assume positions of responsibility, and many go on to become involved in other aspects of community life, for example as school governors. In short, the active involvement of parents in early childhood education can provide appropriate, acceptable and effective parental education – and (for those who need it) access to more formal training in a sympathetic and supportive environment.

5.8   The idea that parents are like professionals in having their own proper competence has important consequences. Like jurors or politicians, parents are ordinary people who undertake a task affecting the whole community. While not all parents can be expected to, or need to, follow one model of parenthood; parents who aspire to competence will seek exemplifications of best practice, wish to ponder the evidence of research, acquire appropriate education and training, and expect other professionals and the community as a whole to fulfil their responsibilities and provide support from the other two points of the triangle of care. These are controversial issues – so much so, that some members of the project's Advisory Committee wish to dissociate themselves from paragraphs 5.8 and 5.9.★ This report seeks to avoid two obvious pitfalls – common heresies expressed by the political left and right: namely, that the problems of contemporary parenthood can be resolved solely by better programmes of assistance (on the one hand), or by more responsible parenthood (on the other). Both are needed. It is not easy to present models of best practice without seeming to criticise those who (for whatever reason) do not, or cannot, conform to them. Some successful parents are non-conformists. But societies need norms, even though not everyone needs to observe them. This report does not criticise either single mothers, gay people, or separated parents. While it is probably true that it is poverty, rather than single parenthood, that is harmful to children, it is also true that poverty is more likely to be the consequence than the cause of single parenthood. In the present state of knowledge, there is a case, not so much for reasserting the traditional model of parenthood (with its pre-determined gender-specific roles), as for promoting a modern version of it (providing flexibility of role), with a mother and father who contract to stay together at least until the (youngest) child reaches the age of parenthood, and who honour the contract.

5.9   Although this is a high ideal increasing evidence suggests that two common alternatives are models which carry high risks for children, single parenthood and broken parenthood. We should not be surprised to discover that fathers are important for children's development and welfare, as well as mothers. Or that the stability of the home is a significant factor. Commonsense, as well as research, suggests that children (both boys and girls) need role-models of both sexes, that parenthood is quite difficult enough even when two partners work together, to discourage those (who have a choice) from embarking on it alone and that broken homes tend to be bad for children. Of course, there are many exceptions to these generalisations. And few people set out on the journey of parenthood with the intention of becoming single parents, or providing their children with a broken home. Most of those who start as parental partners intend to stay together. The advantages – for children and parents – of the collaborative model are obvious. Like jurors and politicians, parents need appropriate education and support; and like jurors and politicians, they don't always

★   Those who have written to express disagreement include K Sylva, Co-Director of the enquiry, L Abbott, P Gammage, M Lochrie, M Mansfield, C Pascal, G Pugh, I Siraj Blatchford and M Taylor.

get it. One of the benefits provided by good pre-school education is the opportunity it gives for parents to learn and develop some of the skills needed for competence in the role. It is also important to ensure that personal and social education within the school curriculum provides a sound basis for competent parenthood. But more is undoubtedly needed: perhaps we should make available regular and systematic training for parents, possibly linked to the provision of child-benefit. The learning parents need, is of course, (like most worthwhile learning) a complex mixture of knowledge, understanding, skill, experience, attitudes and values. Not all of what is needed to become a competent parent in a modern society comes naturally. Lastly, parents need the support of professionals (e.g. teachers, doctors, social workers) and of the whole community. This is dealt with in what follows.

Professionals

5.10   The midwife is the exemplar. She visits the home, shares her expertise, encourages the parents, empowers the mother to bear and tend the child, teaches basic skills of childcare, and departs. Professional midwifery offers a powerful metaphor for the modern professional of any discipline. As health care (in developed as well as developing countries) shifts its focus from curative to preventative strategies, care-workers need to learn to be 'midwives'. Much the same is true for education. The shift of focus from the old idea that initial education was sufficient, towards the principle of lifelong learning, demands from teachers a new recognition of their role as nurturers of autonomous learners. In early childhood this must involve a relationship of partnership and trust with parents (and children). It implies that the home is normally the learning-base, that the parents are the leading educators, that teaching skills are transferable, that learning continues in the absence of professional teachers. Centre-based early learning should be complementary to learning in the home, not a substitute for it.

5.11   The following chapter considers the question of good practice and its implications for the training (and sustaining) of teachers and carers. This one is concerned with the triangle of care and, in particular, the support and help that parents and children need from professionals (and from the community as a whole) if they are to function effectively and thrive. Professional support supplements, without supplanting, the competence of parents – recognising that it is the mark of professionalism to see through the eyes of dispassion, while parenthood requires steady vision through the eyes of love. Professionals need to do more than pay lip-service to the idea that their relationship with parents is a partnership of equals. In giving it reality, they need to recognise the primacy of the home, generously sharing their experience and expertise, always seeking to enable and empower parents and children to become more confident and self-reliant, teaching without condescension, encouraging without fostering dependence, and constantly preparing to depart. Sooner or later, all good teachers and carers demonstrate their professionalism by conducting a skilful campaign of withdrawal.

The community

5.12   Margaret Thatcher's notorious claim that 'there's no such thing as society' belonged to a period when the virtues of independence, self-reliance and individual enterprise were elevated above those of community, co-operation and partnership. A healthy society needs both. Possibly she intended to echo the more balanced statement of W H Auden:

'There is no such thing as the State
And no-one exists alone;
Hunger allows no choice
To the citizen or the police;
We must love one another or die.'

This is nowhere so true as in the family. As children mature slowly towards independence, self-reliance and autonomy, they need to be sustained by the triangle of care, at one point of which stands the community. It is nonsense for governments or individuals to pretend that the raising of children is a wholly private matter, of no concern to – and outside the responsibility of – the whole community. It takes a whole village to educate a child. But the recognition of this truth has interesting consequences of two kinds. It limits the freedom of parents, as it increases the responsibility of the community. Where societies accept responsibilities – for example, for safety at work, the health service, or elementary education – they typically do three things: seek to identify and exemplify good practice; develop policies to encourage its promotion; and use powers of legislation and public funding to regulate and support the activity in question. Parents who wish the community to fulfil its responsibility at the third point of the triangle of care (as it should) should recognise that community support never comes without strings (nor should it). This is an age-old problem. Few societies have succeeded in settling the question exactly where parental freedom should end and community intervention begin. Should parents be free to deny their children pocket money? television? holidays? education? vaccination? blood-transfusions? shelter? life? The answers to questions like this will be found by recognising that rights and responsibilities (for parents or communities) are indivisible.

5.13   In modern urban societies the idea and ideal of community is not so easy to locate and realise as it is in a traditional African (or English) village. In such villages, where external travel and communication are difficult, communities are strong and neighbourliness thrives. Shared values are derived from an established faith. Extended families are common; people know one another; privacy is rare. (The flip side of good neighbours is busybodies.) But the world of Miss Marple is vanishing. In any event, the parable of the Good Samaritan teaches that it is the stranger who is one's neighbour. Urban societies have found it difficult to develop organic networks of neighbours and living communities which can provide support for their shifting populations. They tend to replace the 'natural community' of village life with the structures of government. But these are inevitably defined by location (borough, county, region, country ...) and find it difficult to serve people who less and less define themselves as belonging to a place. The urban parish is in decay. It is interesting – but not surprising – that the resurgence of nationalism coincides with a period of history where the experience of the diaspora is becoming almost universal. So the concept of community presents a double challenge: how can we organise urban society into effective units for (self) government? and how can natural communities develop within the shifting populations of modern life? For some, the idea of community is best represented in groups with a shared place of work (like a coalmine or a college or a company), or a shared expertise or interest (like a profession or a club or a church). For others, the local community still generates effective groups, such as the neighbourhood watch or pre-school playgroup. There are different kinds of community and many possible forms of community support for parents. One of the most interesting is provided by the new world-wide movement towards the concept of 'learning cities' (see Hirsch, 1993, *Cities for Learning*, and Woolhouse, forthcoming). The 'learning city' is expected to meet ten basic criteria of which the fourth is:

> 'to promote and set up, if necessary, the possibility of specialised training for parents in the education of their children and offer young people before adulthood new perspectives, new horizons in a changing world that neither the family nor the schools are in a position to give them and which they cannot develop themselves.' (OECD/ CERI, 1993).

5.14   What kind of support do parents seek and need from the community? It has been suggested above that they need help of four kinds to begin with: the identification and exemplification of good practice in parenthood, the encouragement and support of good practice by appropriate social policies, the provision of parental education (and also, perhaps, training) and the reorientation of the relevant professions to enable them to work in partnership with parents. Parents also expect the community to provide a good learning environment in which their children can grow up. But, beyond those needs, there are the three kinds of support that were set out in paragraph 1.17 as desirable and necessary: the introduction of paid parental leave; a recognition that provision for the care of pre-school children of employed parents is a responsibility which should be shared between parents, employers and the public, but requires leadership from the Government; and – the major concern of this report – the provision of high quality pre-school education for all children from the age of three.

Conclusions

5.15   This review of the roles of the home and the community (and of professionals) in the promotion of good early learning leads to the following *conclusions*:

a) children are most likely to thrive (and learn) in a secure triangle of care provided by parents, professionals and the community as a whole;

b) the role of parents is the most important for the welfare of the child;

c) parents should be thought of – and should learn to think of themselves – as aspiring to competence in a role which requires preparation, study and reflection, like any demanding work;

d) parents are children's first and most important educators;

e) like all good teachers, parents should strive to be 'warm demanders';

f) confidence is an important quality in successful parenting, but parents need help in developing and sustaining confidence;

g) what is needed is a real partnership between parents and professionals;

h) parental involvement in early childhood education is a key feature of high-quality provision, and yields multiple benefits to the parents as well as the children;

i) parents need exemplifications of different forms of good practice, information about the findings of research, appropriate education and the effective support of professionals and the community as a whole;

j) modern professionals seek to follow the example of midwives, who (conscious of their supporting role) share expertise and experience, seek to foster self-reliance and confidence, and know how to withdraw gracefully;

k) the whole community has an interest in, and a responsibility for, the welfare and early learning of children;

l) there is an urgent need for (i) the introduction of paid parental leave; (ii) a recognition that provision for the care of pre-school children of employed parents is a responsibility which should be shared between parents, employers and the public – with the Government offering a lead; (iii) the provision of high-quality pre-school education for all children from the age of three.

5.16   It is therefore *recommended* that:

5 the churches, religious and community leaders should stimulate a major public debate on the subject of parenthood in order to establish exemplifications of good practice based on research and proven experience;

6 the Government should consider how parents can be given access to systematic and appropriate education and support to enable them to fulfil their roles most effectively;

7 professional bodies and institutions of training concerned with early childhood care and education should review their training and practice to ensure that they offer parents a real partnership;

8 the Government should consider its position in relation to (a) paid parental leave, (b) the care of pre-school children of employed parents, and (c) pre-school education, and take steps to enable the community to fulfil its responsibilities in each of these areas.

6. Good Practice

'Do all the good you can,
By all the means you can,
In all the ways you can,
In all the places you can,
At all the times you can,
To all the people you can,
As long as ever you can.'

(John Wesley's *Rule*)

This chapter discusses the nature of good practice and high-quality provision for early learning. It argues that quality depends on a set of principles, not a favoured type of provision. It sets out twelve principles as the fundamentals of good practice, and derives from these ten common features which can serve as guidelines for good early learning in group settings or in the home. They include well-trained staff, appropriate adult-child ratios, suitable curriculum, adequate resources, parent participation, diverse peer groups, a multi-professional approach. The UK lacks adequate arrangements for quality review and assurance. There is a need for a clear national lead and a new legislative framework, backed by resources, to meet the needs of children and parents. The quality of early learning depends on the quality of teachers and carers. Their education, training and continuing professional development need attention. In particular, recognition should be given to the special responsibility and competence required of early years graduate teachers. There are two recommendations calling for an authoritative Code of Conduct and a review of the training of early years teachers.

Introduction

6.1   Previous chapters have emphasised the importance of quality to the effectiveness of pre-school education. The identification of high-quality provision depends on a range of factors: for example, the involvement of parents (more accurately, *partnership with parents*) is known both from research and experience to be essential (see Chapters 2 and 5). But there are also other factors. In Chapter 2 it was concluded that *quality* might be defined in terms of (a) a curriculum based on active learning or 'purposeful play', (b) the selection, training, retention and ratio of staff, (c) parental involvement, (d) buildings and equipment, (e) diversity of the peer group.

6.2   This report takes the view that the quality of provision for early learning depends on a set of principles, rather than upon a favoured type. Neither nursery schools nor playgroups, for example, are inherently of high quality; but each may be so, if they adhere to the principles of quality and observe good practice. The diverse pattern of provision in the UK makes it all the more important to establish guidelines against which the quality of learning in early childhood settings may be evaluated. We need to know what constitutes 'good practice', if the quality and effectiveness of early learning is to be enhanced. This chapter seeks to identify a well-defined, but flexible, framework of principles and guidelines based on an informed understanding of how young children learn most effectively, which can serve to promote and sustain good early learning.

Fundamental principles

6.3   There are twelve principles which are fundamental to good practice. They are not new; indeed, they are exemplified by the work of Tina Bruce (1987) *Early Childhood Education* and the Early Years Curriculum Group (1992) *First Things First: Educating Young Children*. Nor are they solely applicable to early childhood. In many cases they apply with equal force to the learning of adolescents or adults.

   i.   **Early childhood is the foundation on which children build the rest of their lives. But it is not just a preparation for adolescence and adulthood: it has an importance in itself.** One of the skills of parenthood and childcare is to help children strike a balance between the experience of the full life of childhood and the preparation for later stages of life. This is not easy. It is not just a question of remembering that some children do not survive childhood (Beth in *Little Women* or Jo in *Bleak House* are exemplars), but can nonetheless be fully human. It involves recognising that children have rights and proper roles, as much as adults do. The United Nations *Convention on the Rights of the Child* and the UK Children Act 1989 have each emphasised this principle. Sometimes in the past, societies have appeared to suggest to children that the only virtues they can hope to achieve are patience and restraint: the rest must wait for adulthood. This is wrong. The cardinal virtues (such as justice, prudence or hope) and the fruit of the spirit (such as gentleness, joy or peace) are as accessible to children as adults – if not more so. Violence is a sign of an unlived life; delinquency of an unfulfilled childhood.

   ii.   **Children develop at different rates, and in different ways, – emotionally, intellectually, morally, socially, physically and spiritually. All are important; each is interwoven with others.** Professor Howard Gardner argues that there is not just one kind of intelligence, but seven: linguistic, logical, musical, physical, visual/spatial, inter-personal and intra-personal ('know thyself'). (See *Creating the Future*, 1991, pages 68-75.) Nursery schools, building on the analysis of domains of learning originally contributed by Her Majesty's Inspectorate, often recognise a curricular range which also includes seven components: aesthetic and creative (e.g. art and music), human and social (e.g. relationships, environment, cultures, history), language and literacy (e.g. listening, speaking, reading, writing), mathematics (e.g. shape, number, measuring, sorting, assessing, recording), physical (e.g. bodily and spatial awareness, physical skills and imagination, bodily knowledge, health and safety, social interaction), science and technology (e.g. life and its environment, materials and their properties, energy, force, time, space, weather, use of materials, tools, planning and construction), moral and spiritual (e.g. self-awareness, right and wrong, fairness, human variety, tolerance, wonder, responsibility). The richness of these analyses is notable; so is their interpenetration.

iii. **All children have abilities which can (and should be) identified and promoted.** If this principle causes surprise to any readers, let me urge them to investigate the learning of children with special educational needs. No-one denies that humans vary in learning-speed: there are slower and faster learners. Nor that talent and aptitude is unevenly distributed among the seven intelligences of particular individuals, or between individuals. But no-one has none. And most children have a 'best subject', a favourite sport, a special hobby or a particular skill – which can provide the starting-point for wider learning. Those who doubt this should not become teachers.

iv. **Young children learn from everything that happens to them and around them; they do not separate their learning into different subjects or disciplines.** In this respect, young children are no different to most adults who, once they have completed their schooling and college education, tend to revert to integrated learning. It is the traditional (and increasingly unsatisfactory) map of learning representing separate subjects and distinct disciplines that is unnatural, not the human instinct for integrated learning. Early learning takes place both formally and informally, at home and at school, with adults and with other children, in company and alone. Good practice recognises and uses the diversity of experience which contributes to the integrated learning of childhood.

v. **Children learn most effectively through actions, rather than from instruction.** Are adults different? Learning from instruction is an advanced and difficult skill, which some people never acquire. The theory of learning styles suggests that people may have different preferred styles of learning. Some learn well through seeing, others by hearing, and a third group learn best when they can touch and feel and handle. The importance of all our senses to learning can be seen by watching a baby learn by putting things in its mouth, or recalling the evocative power of smell. Young children, in particular, need to engage all their senses in the process of learning; for them, learning is doing.

vi. **Children learn best when they are actively involved and interested.** Motivation is one of the prerequisites of learning; confidence is the other. Get your wanting right – and all else will follow. The first task of the teacher or parent is motivation. In young children it is usually brimming over and abundant; good teaching involves harnessing, directing and focusing the powerful motivation of early learners, without frustrating or dampening it.

vii. **Children who feel confident in themselves and their own ability have a head-start to learning.** Confidence is more like being able to dance than the possession of brown eyes: it can be learned and developed. The encouragement and nurturing of confidence in children are among the first and most important responsibilities of parents and teachers.

viii. **Children need time and space to produce work of quality and depth.** On the one hand, this principle has obvious implications for the environment and equipment that is needed to support early learning. On the other, it suggests that nine or ten hours a week may not provide sufficient centre-based learning to satisfy a child's needs. The evidence of research supports the conclusion that regular half-day pre-school education is adequate; less is not, more may be unnecessary.

ix. **What children can do (rather than what they cannot do) is the starting point in their learning.** There are two reasons for this. One is the enormous importance of confidence in learning. Competence breeds confidence. Few people have much self-confidence in areas where they know nothing, or are wholly lacking in skill. The other reason has to do with the concept of 'readiness' (experience of learning 'appropriate to age and individuality'). Children learn to walk and talk when they are ready to do so: it is a mistake to try to make them learn those skills before they are ready. The principle of 'learning readiness' (to be understood as a gradual process rather than a precise stage) has a wide application, as the Carnegie Foundation's study, *Ready to Learn* (1991), has argued, and probably extends well beyond early childhood.

x. **Play and conversation are the main ways by which young children learn about themselves, other people and the world around them.** It is obvious that children deprived of the opportunity to play and converse do not thrive. It is difficult to over-estimate the importance of those activities. Play is children's work. And questioning is an essential feature of their healthy development. Early learning will be impeded, if not prevented, where children are not encouraged to play and talk.

xi. **Children who are encouraged to think for themselves are more likely to act independently.** This is obvious, but its importance may not be. One of the harmful results of much traditional education is learning-dependence, the apparent inability to learn unaided. It is an unnatural, as well as a regrettable, condition – as the most casual study of infants reveals. Babies learn voraciously, aided or unaided; though (of course) they do best when encouraged, supported and helped. There is no doubt that lifelong learning will be required of us all in the twenty-first century – it is already desirable – and that the task of initial education, therefore, is to prepare young people for mature, independent, autonomous learning. If these qualities are not fostered and developed in early childhood, they become progressively more difficult to achieve.

xii **The relationships which children make with other children and with adults are of central importance to their development.** This is not only because of the importance of the development of Gardner's 'inter-personal intelligence' (the qualities that enable us to 'get on' with other people) and the central role of teamwork and other inter-personal skills in modern life. It also derives from the fact that most people learn best in the presence of 'warm demanders', teachers (or parents, or peers) who provide a stimulating mix of security and challenge (see 5.3). Indeed, most learners (young or mature) need three different kinds of security (relational, contextual and conceptual) to help them succeed. We need people we are comfortable with, a secure learning environment and an understanding of how what is to be learned 'fits' into our existing conceptual framework. This last quality is sometimes called 'field-dependence' – the desire to see the whole picture before studying part of it and the need to grasp the personal relevance of what is being learned. Field-independent learning is relatively rare: if it develops at all, it comes late to most people. But regrettably much of traditional education is presented as if field-independent learning were natural and normal.

Common features

6.4   What constitutes good practice in the early years is well established. Research evidence, policy documents and observed practice throughout the developed world agree on the features which characterise good practice in all early childhood settings, both for centre-based learning and in the home. (See Pascal and Bertram, 1991, *Defining and Assessing Quality in the Education of Children from Four to Seven Years* and The Early Years Curriculum Group, 1992, *First Things First*.) The first requirement is the establishment of *clear aims and objectives*. There needs to be a shared understanding among all the educating adults (parents and professionals of all kinds), and between the adults and the children, of what they are aiming to achieve. It is not enough to establish a clear set of aims: they need to be openly and regularly discussed – and opportunities should be provided for everyone involved in the learning process (children and adults) to shape and modify the aims.

6.5   The second requirement is a *broad, balanced and developmentally appropriate curriculum*. This should be so planned as to foster the all-round development of individual children – emotionally, intellectually, morally, socially, physically and spiritually. The nature of the early years curriculum has already been examined in earlier parts of this report (see, especially, 2.16 – 17 and 6.3(ii)). It has been argued that early learning provides an essential 'foundation stage' for the school curriculum, and for adult learning. As with all education, successful early learning requires educators who expect children to gain specific knowledge, skills and attitudes through the curriculum that is offered. There is a vital link between the expectations of educators (including and especially the parents) and the aspirations of students. Educators should provide a variety of learning experience and increase the difficulty and challenge of each activity, as they observe the child's developing understanding and skill. Consequently, the curriculum provides both continuity and progression for each individual child. Appendix E discusses the curriculum in greater detail.

6.6   The fourth Foundation Target (of the National Training and Education Targets) calls for 'the development of self-reliance, flexibility and breadth'. These qualities, which are among the 'super-skills' of learning (see 2.16), lie at the heart of the early years curriculum. Self-reliance permits responsible learning and lays the basis for the development of mature, independent, autonomous learners. Flexibility – or adaptability – is the quality that enables people to survive, tolerate, and (at the best) embrace change. Humans are set apart from most other species by their extraordinary adaptability; among humans this quality significantly distinguishes successful people from those who are less successful. It can be learned and developed: those who lack flexibility are disabled. Breadth is the quality that enables us to make connections – the basis of intelligence. It can be defined in a number of ways: the development of all seven of Gardner's multiple intelligences; the exploration of each 'domain of learning' (see 6.3 (ii)); an education which balances the six types of learning – knowledge, understanding, skills, experience, attitudes, values; or (as the opposite of narrowness) the study of a wide range of subjects, disciplines or occupational vocations. But there are other 'super skills' and attributes, no less important than these. In particular, the early years curriculum is centrally concerned with motivation, confidence and socialisation – without which learning is hardly possible at all. These are cold words: Langland's 'Holy Church' (personified in *Piers Plowman* rather as if she were a nursery-school teacher) sums up the curriculum in this way, 'Learn to love, and leave all other'.

6.7   The third requirement is *a variety of learning experiences which are active, relevant and enjoyable*. This involves an emphasis on learning as an interactive process and demands educators who give support to children's learning through active exploration and interaction with adults, other children, ideas and materials. Good practice requires:

* provision of many and varied opportunities for children and adults to talk and communicate about learning;
* learning activities which are concrete, real and relevant to the lives of young children;
* educators who acknowledge and utilise purposeful play as a powerful medium for learning;
* adults who support and develop each child's self-esteem and identity, involve themselves in learning activities and extend children's learning by asking and answering questions, and by stimulating the child's curiosity, imagination and wonder;
* opportunities for children to choose from a variety of activities, materials and equipment;
* provision for large groups, small groups, individual and solitary activities;
* outdoor experience on a daily basis;
* periods of uninterrupted time to enable children to explore and engage in activities according to individual interest and involvement;
* a balance of movement and rest in the daily programme;
* an achieved aim of ensuring that learning is fun.

6.8   The fourth requirement for good practice is the *development of warm and positive relationships*. Children need to feel welcome, secure and valued, if they are to learn effectively at home or in group settings. (See 5.3 and 6.3) Above all, good practice requires a consistent and (ideally) shared understanding of behavioural expectations, codes of conduct and values for all (adults and children alike) in the home or group setting.

6.9   The fifth requirement is a *well-planned, stimulating, secure and healthy environment*. The learning environment should provide a variety of learning experiences indoors and out, space for movement and small, intimate areas for rest and quiet; it should provide equipment and resources to reflect the children's range of development and to promote early learning through purposeful play. While the environment should provide a place for the personal belongings of each child and adult (and an area for adults to have to themselves), it should as a whole be 'owned' by the children and organised so as to be accessible to them in such a way as to promote their growing independence and autonomy.

6.10   The sixth requirement is a *commitment to equal opportunities and social justice* for all. All children should be able to take a full and active part in high-quality early education both at home and in pre-school centre-based learning. The learning environment and experience should reflect and value each child's family, home, culture, language and beliefs; and encourage a respect for – and appreciation of – the rich variety of communities in our multi-faceted culture. All children should be treated fairly and in a non-discriminatory way. They should be provided with positive role models and activities which challenge stereotyping and discrimination. Parents and professional educators should seek to adopt a positive stance in the promotion of equal opportunities and in countering prejudice and injustice, whether derived from race, culture, (dis)ability, class or gender. Each is important, but the issue of gender needs special attention. The lack of men in early childhood settings needs to be addressed. So long as societies arrange for the caring for young children – as distinct from the bearing of them – to be seen as 'women's work', we shall not achieve social justice, nor provide appropriate role models for children. This issue affects the status, pay and career structure of those who work with young children. But is also has implications for parenthood. Where (as for many children at present) the home cannot offer opportunities for close and lasting relationships with adults of both sexes, it will be important to seek to provide for them in other ways. Here is a further function for good centre-based early learning, with the obvious implication that there should be a reasonable gender-balance in the staffing.

6.11   There are also four further requirements for good practice which apply predominantly or wholly to group settings in which early learning takes place. They are set out briefly here, but each of them has important implications for the education and training of teachers and carers of young children, an important issue which is addressed in the next section of this Chapter.

    (a)   *Systematic planning, assessment, and record keeping.*
- planning based on regular and systematic observation of children and a study of each child's individual development, special interests and progress;
- compilation of individual records for children, including contributions from, and shared with, both parents and children;
- decisions made on the basis of a wide range of information gathered from a variety of sources, of which the parents are the most important;
- early identification of children with special needs or at risk.

    (b)   *Satisfactory adult:child ratios, continuity of care, and consistent staff development* (cf. Chapter 3).
- adult:child ratios which permit close and effective contact and interaction (cf. the RSA rule of thumb set out in 3.16);
- small groups which encourage the development of positive relationships;
- appropriate and on-going development and training for all adults involved in centre-based learning (including parents);
- stability, consistency, and continuity among those who work in group settings;
- a balance between men and women staff.

    (c)   *Partnership with parents and families; liaison with the community* (cf. Chapter 5).
- recognition and valuing of parents as children's primary educators;
- sharing with parents the decisions about their children's care and education;
- seeking active parental involvement in children's learning experiences;
- frequent, regular, and reciprocal contacts with parents, and communication about children's individual needs and progress;
- regular liaison with both the home and other community providers and support agencies about the development of individual children, their experience and needs;
- co-ordination and transfer of information at each transitional point in a child's early learning (especially at entry to pre-school, and at the point of transition to primary education).

    (d)   *Effective procedures for monitoring and evaluating the quality of practice.*
- established procedures for the regular and systematic monitoring and assessment of the quality of early education in group settings;
- involvement of all participants in these procedures – including managers, staff, parents and children;
- encouragement of systematic and regular self-assessment and review;
- following up the evaluation process with action designed to improve the quality of early education in the group setting.

6.12   The previous paragraphs have set out a summary of what is well established and widely recognised as good practice. These guidelines could be developed to form a Code of Conduct for good practice in early learning. A number of current initiatives are seeking to do this, e.g. the Worcester College project, the Early Childhood Forum project, and the Early Years Curriculum Group. (The topic is usefully addressed in Bertram and Pascal, forthcoming, *Developing a Quality Curriculum for Young Children*.) The diverse pattern of provision in the UK, however, makes it difficult to ascertain and monitor the quality of learning experiences offered to young children. There is a lack of thorough and systematic quality review, and a need for appropriate and rigorous procedures for quality development and assurance for all centre-based early learning. One of the purposes of a national evaluation of the diversity of provision would be to enable parents to make informed choices. At present, there are no effective incentives to encourage the evaluation of quality and the pursuit of strategies of improvement. There needs to be a clear lead at national level to acknowledge the importance of establishing high-quality early learning experiences, to raise the status of work with young children, and to confirm that good practice demands quality before quantity of provision. There is a need for a coherent national policy and a consistent legislative framework to resolve the existing tensions and contradictions created by the Children Act 1989 and the Education Reform Act 1988 (and subsequent legislation). But high-quality and effective early learning for all young children will not come cheaply. While substantial benefits can be expected, there is no doubt that substantial investment is needed. While the next Chapter explores the issue of funding, and proposes a practical programme of reform, there remains one feature of good practice that is so fundamental that it requires separate treatment: the quality of early years professionals.

Teachers and carers

6.13 Together with the role of parents and the nature of the curriculum, the calibre and training of the professionals who work with children are the key determinants of high-quality provision. There are several kinds of professions involved in childcare and early learning. There are three broad spheres of activity: care, health and education; three sectors of provision: public, private and voluntary; and a variety of professional groups involved – including teachers, nursery nurses, playgroup workers and childminders. Each service has its distinct ethos, aims and patterns of training; yet they need to be able to work together to achieve quality and to enable an effective use of available resources.

6.14 The Rumbold Report looked for 'a closer linkage between the three strands of health, care and education in initial and in-service training; a pattern of vocational training and qualifications for childcare workers which will bridge the gap between vocational and academic qualifications; safeguarding both the rigour and relevance of initial training of teachers ...; and affording improved opportunities of in-service training for childcare workers in educational settings'. (*Starting with Quality*, 1990). This linkage implies the idea of a professional continuum stretching from the parent on one side to the graduate early-years teacher at the other. Within the continuum there needs to be a clear and well-articulated structure of education and training in all aspects of professional responsibility centred on the education of the young child. This must include provision for continuing professional development at each stage. This continuum can be seen as a series of interlocking stages in which adults reach successive levels of competence on the basis of which their further professional development can take place. Within the continuum (and as part of the team) there will be a variety of early childhood professionals, with different specialisms and training, but all possessing a common core of knowledge and understanding which can be differently deployed and gradually extended. The 'common core' characteristics of early years professionals include: practice based on knowledge and understanding of cognitive, linguistic, social, emotional and physical development; skill in the creation of a curriculum tailored to individual children based on understanding of child development, play and active learning; good observational, social and communication skills; a code of professional ethics including child advocacy. Such professionals can progress at their own pace, as they acquire further levels of competence and understanding. The idea of a professional continuum is not only of benefit to children, but also a way of ensuring that adults with high potential to develop professionally are not frustrated, or turned away from work with children.

6.15 Nonetheless, the standards of training and qualifications should remain high at each stage. Working with young children is a complex and demanding task – it requires a team of professionals who are appropriately trained to adopt a variety of roles and responsibilities. The team may include nursery nurses, parents, managers, teachers, health care and special needs staff and ancillaries. The training for each worker will not be the same nor will each require the same length or depth of training but every member will have an important and significant role to play. There should be opportunities for team members to share some aspects of training but the team should be led (but not necessarily *managed*) by a graduate who has undergone rigorous training and has gained a degree in the Early Childhood field. This may be a B.Ed. or B.A. leading to qualified teacher status, PGCE, or multidisciplinary degree such as the new B.A. Early Childhood Studies degree. Following the public outcry against the suggestion that a 'mums' army' should be recruited to teach young children, the proposal was withdrawn and the graduate status of Early Years teachers reaffirmed. The new proposals for training classroom assistants to work alongside teachers will necessitate courses of high quality which can be recognised as part of the professional continuum.

6.16 A ladder of progression or continuum of learning, established on a nationwide basis would allow entry, exit and take-up at appropriate points in order to meet the needs of the individual and the establishment in which they work. Some of the rungs of this ladder are now in place, or being shaped. The recently established system of National (or Scottish) Vocational Qualifications (NVQ or SVQ) in Community Care and in Child Care and Education provides a framework for accrediting workers in the care and early education fields. A framework for professional development overseen by the Council for Accreditation of Child Care and Education would allow for progression from levels 2 and 3 of NVQ/SVQ to higher education. The new B.A. in Early Childhood Studies (for example) provides opportunities for those who do not possess standard entry requirements for a degree course to claim accreditation for prior experience or learning (APEL). This means that, whilst rigorous entry procedures must be followed, access is widened to include routes other than standard 'A' level entry. The Rumbold report argued that the increase in pre-school provision by the private and voluntary sector and concern on the part of Local Authorities to safeguard the quality of early childhood experiences point to the need for both recognition of the skill and competence of those in the workplace and access to training and professional qualifications for those who wish to acquire further knowledge and skill through attendance on a course. This is all the more important because research evidence is pointing increasingly to the critical relationship between the level and appropriateness of the training received by staff and the quality of the provision for which they are responsible.

6.17 The professional preparation of teachers is complex because teaching itself is complex. This is true for teachers at all stages. But it has been argued earlier in this report (3.15) that early years teachers require a breadth of knowledge, understanding and experience which is not required by those training to teach older children. The early years constitute a crucial stage in which the foundations for later learning are laid. A vast amount of learning and development takes place during these early years and teachers must be fully equipped to capture the unreturning moment. They must have mastery of the curriculum content as well as having a sound knowledge of child development including language acquisition, cognitive, social, emotional and physical development. They are required to lead and plan for a team of other professionals including parents, nursery nurses, students, and others including speech therapists, language support teachers, psychologists and social workers. They are responsible for the assessment of children and for monitoring progress and ensuring continuity and progression between stages and establishments. It is widely recognised that the quality of children's education depends on the quality of the teachers, and the effectiveness of their training and development. Training for teachers in the early years should not be any less rigorous or demanding than that of any other teacher.

6.18   To be professional is to do more than exhibit a collection of narrow competences, like someone playing 'noughts and crosses' or making toast. The broad competence of the professional includes reflection, 'being as well as doing', and continuous development. Above all, it implies actions which are derived from a theoretical approach to the task and which reflect explicit and shared professional values. These three levels of competence – practical teaching skill, a theoretical grasp of learning, and secure professional values – are required of all teachers, but are particularly important to early childhood education. There are two reasons for this. The first has to do with content, the second with learning development. It takes no less a sophisticated understanding of, say, the nature of science, or language, to interpret it to young children, than to older ones. Indeed, in some respects, sophisticated and sensitive interpretation of knowledge and its careful matching to a child's needs and abilities provide greater challenges to academic and pedagogical ability. Moreover, as early learning constitutes a distinct stage of learning and provides an essential foundation for what comes later, early childhood teachers need to understand a theory of learning development, including the concept of 'readiness' (the match between a child's level of skill and the task at hand), and be able to apply this to the wide variety of children in their care. Their knowledge of learning development is the heart of their professionalism: it demands just as subtle and complex an understanding as the mastery of disciplines that is demanded of teachers in schools, colleges or universities.

Conclusions

6.19   This review of the nature of good practice leads to the following *conclusions*:
   a) quality of early learning depends on a set of principles, not a favoured type of provision;
   b) there are twelve principles which are fundamental to good practice;
   c) from these may be derived a set of ten common features which serve as guidelines for good early learning in group settings or in the home;
   d) these principles and guidelines are well established and widely recognised as the components of good practice – which may be summarised in the following list of essential criteria for high-quality educational provision for young children:
      i.   well-trained staff led by a graduate teacher
      ii.   appropriate adult:child ratios (cf. the RSA 'rule of thumb', 3.16)

    iii. suitable curriculum

    iv. adequate resources

    v. participation of parents

    vi. diverse peer group

    vii. a multi-professional approach;

e) the diverse pattern of provision in the UK lacks adequate arrangements for quality review and quality assurance;

f) for these and other reasons, there is a need for a clear national lead and new legislative framework, backed up with appropriate funding, to ensure that all young children are provided with opportunities for good pre-school education, and that parents are able to make well-informed choices;

g) the quality of early learning depends on the quality of teachers and carers, the curriculum and the role of parents;

h) there is a professional continuum stretching from parents on one side to graduate (early years) teachers on the other;

i) training and professional development of high quality needs to be available at each step along the professional continuum;

j) the professional teacher has acquired the practical skills of teaching, a theoretical understanding of learning (within and across subjects), and secure professional values;

k) early years teachers require a double competence: the ability to interpret the complexities of (for example) science or language in a form accessible to young children, and the mastery of a theory of learning development which they can apply to the diversity of children in their care.

6.20   Accordingly, it is *recommended* that:

9 **early years practitioners should draw up an authoritative Code of Conduct based on the principles and guidelines for good practice set out in this report;**

10 **the Department for Education should review its plans for the professional development and training of early years teachers in the light of the claims made in this report, that:**

  a) **the curriculum of early learning forms a fundamental, distinct and essential phase of education, without which it is difficult for children to progress successfully in school or into adult learning;**

  b) **the double competence required of early years teachers – especially the mastery of an applicable theory of learning development – makes just as intense a professional demand on students as does the mastery of disciplines required of all teachers;**

  c) **the training and development of early years teachers should be no less rigorous and demanding than that appropriate to any other teachers.**

7. Realising the Vision: a Practical Programme

'The success of any great moral enterprise does not depend on numbers'

(William Lloyd Garrison, 1805-79)

This chapter seeks to offer a practical programme for achieving the objective of providing good pre-school education for all children. It identifies the underlying problem as one of finance – or rather of our implicit national priorities. It puts the cost of the required programme at between £600 million and £900 million a year. Substantial new funding for pre-school education can be justified by arguments from investment, priorities and the relative value of early learning. A new solution to the problem is outlined, including raising the age at which children start compulsory full-time schooling from five to six. The potential advantages of such a change are described. The question of whether pre-school education should be compulsory is raised. Responsibility for early learning must be clearly located in one place, perhaps (for the time being) by the creation of a special Commission. On the assumption that the new provision is to be gradually introduced between 1994 and 1999, the necessary transitional arrangements are reviewed. There are seven recommendations addressed to the RSA and other bodies, but especially to the Government.

Introduction

7.1   Much of what is set out in Chapters 2 – 6 has been said and written before. The problem is not so much to identify what is needed, as to find a way of providing it. The campaign for early learning in the UK has continually demonstrated the truth of Viscount Morley's aphorism: 'success depends on three things: who says it, what he says, how he says it; and of these three things, what he says is the least important'. The Prime Minister has asserted that the Government is 'determined that every child in this country should have the best start in life' (*Choice and Diversity: a new framework for schools*, 1992). However, Kenneth Clarke, Chancellor of the Exchequer, told the North of England Education Conference in 1991, when he was Secretary of State for Education, that nursery education for all was 'not a realistic prospect'. What are we to make of this apparent contradiction?

7.2   These two statements could be reconciled, if one were to suppose that the Government believed *either* that the evidence of research has not yet demonstrated the value of good early learning, *or* that the existing pattern of provision in the UK provides 'the best start in life' for every child. In fact, it has at times appeared to hold both these beliefs. This report has set out the reasons for thinking that each is incorrect. Chapter 2 (and appendix C) has presented the evidence of research: while it needs to be further developed and tested, it is already firm enough to be persuasive. Chapter 4 examined existing provision in the UK and concluded that the position is seriously inadequate. Neither defence is any longer sustainable. But there remains a third impediment to progress: money. No one denies that the provision of good opportunities for early learning for all children will be expensive. Ministers understandably challenge those who promote the public provision of pre-school education to explain where the funds are to be found, and at what cost to other programmes. That challenge must now be faced.

7.3   But, before turning to the issue of funding, it is important to be clear about what is required. Paragraph 1.17 of this report set out a clear programme – covering paid parental leave, arrangements for the care of the pre-school children of those in employment, the education and support of parents, and an entitlement to good early learning for all children from the age of three. All four are needed, and each gives support to the others. But this report's detailed proposals are confined to the fourth item – that all children should be enabled to 'start right' in learning outside as well as within the home. The other three items will also require further funding, if they are to become systematically available. But it must be left to others, such as the Equal Opportunities Commission, to develop detailed proposals. In any event, in the case of the first two (parental leave and the care of children of those in employment) it would be appropriate to design a system of mixed funding, drawing contributions from public funds, the employers and employees in an appropriate balance – on the principle of requiring those who benefit to pay. Where benefits are distributed, responsibility for funding should accordingly be shared. But there is even more work to be done in connection with the third item, the education and support of parents. While recognising that this is a difficult and controversial area, this report has repeatedly identified a need for the UK to give more attention to the education and support of parents. While the theme is not further pursued here, there are several major issues for others to grapple with: the nature of the education and support required, the timing of the provision, the allocation of responsibility for delivery, the costs and coverage of any system, and so on. It is hoped that others will find practical answers to these questions.

7.4   The RSA project has sought to develop a shared national target, that no child born after the year 2000 in the UK should be deprived of opportunity and support for effective early learning. This will require new legislation. What is sought is a statutory and mandatory responsibility to provide free, high-quality, half-day early learning for all children aged three to four by not later than the year 2000; and that such provision should be adequately resourced and set in an appropriate context of care and support. While recognising that 'learning' and 'care' cannot be artificially separated, one practical path to this objective would be legislation requiring Local Authorities to provide extended daycare for all three- to four-year-olds (whose parents wanted it) on a basis which integrated half-day early learning (free) with half-day extended care (charged for on a means-tested fee-paying basis). It is assumed that Local Authorities would build on the diverse pattern of provision which is already in place, and make gradual progress towards the objective, which would be linked to a target date at or close to the turn of the century. While in the transitional period many compromises would be required, the legislation must enshrine four essential principles: that the entitlement is available to all children, is free (as far as the half-day early learning is concerned), is of high-quality, and achieves the integration of early learning and daycare (for those parents who require and pay for the latter). What would this cost, and how could it be paid for?

Funding

7.5   There are three estimates available at present of the costs of such a programme. Setting aside the extended daycare element (or assuming that the means-tested fees were set at a level to ensure that it was largely self-financing), those who have investigated the question broadly agree that a sum of between half- and one-billion pounds a year is required. A recent Ministerial statement quotes an estimate from the Department for Education of 'over half-a-billion pounds a year' (together with 'substantial capital costs') for 'forcing the State to provide a place for every three- and four-year-old, irrespective of parental income'. Sally Holtermann's masterly study for the National Children's Bureau sets the figure at £450 million, *including* £100 million of capital expenditure (Holtermann, 1992, *Investing in Young Children: costing an education and day care service*). The National Commission more recently reached a figure of £860 million for the recurrent costs of the expansion of nursery education proposed in *Learning to Succeed* (see appendix G). Given that these estimates probably related to slightly different programmes of provision, were made in different years, and were designed for different purposes, their convergence is remarkable. What is required is a recurrent sum of the order of £600 - £900 million.

7.6   There are three main arguments for seeking substantial new funding for nursery education. They are the arguments from investment, priorities, and relative value. In Chapter 2 it was argued that investment in high-quality early education provides a worthwhile economic return to society, and evidence was set out in support of this claim. In Chapter 4 it was argued that while funding appears to be a major impediment to progress, in reality the problem is one of priorities, and that pre-school education should be among a nation's first priorities. Chapter 1 introduced the idea that resources in education need to be tilted back towards early learning; and elsewhere the report has repeatedly quoted the RSA 'rule of thumb' for staff:pupil/student ratios which proposes that class sizes should be roughly equivalent to twice the average age of the learners. Such a principle (if adopted) would significantly shift resources back towards early learning without necessarily making a substantial demand for new funds on the education budget. (However, the transition period would need extra funds, since it would be a mistake to increase ratios in secondary and tertiary education until the pupils who had experienced the reformed and more generous provision in nursery and primary education entered the more advanced phase.)

7.7   Each of these arguments has weight: each is addressed to a different audience. The argument from investment is presented to the Chancellor of the Exchequer and the Treasury; the argument from priorities to parliament; the argument from relative value to the Secretary of State and the Department for Education. To those Ministers who ask how nursery education is to be paid for, and at what cost to other programmes, it is answered that the argument from investment shows that the costs will be recouped over time, that (until that happens) the argument from priorities places nursery education above most other programmes of public provision, which therefore should release the sums required (if increases in taxation are ruled out), but that a rebalancing of the educational budget in favour of early learning could ultimately provide most of what is required at the expense of the gradual introduction of higher staff:pupil/student ratios in later secondary and post-school education. (Such higher ratios would prove to be manageable and effective as and when the cohorts of students who had received good pre-school education matured and progressed.) Moreover, the earlier RSA report, *More Means Different* (RSA, 1990) offered a strategy for funding higher education through greater reliance on private funding ('top-up' fees payable by students and not recouped from public funds), which is still under consideration. The adoption of such an approach to higher education could also play a role in the rebalancing of the educational budget.

7.8   One of the subordinate, but still important, points to be considered in relation to the funding of systematic pre-school education is whether the resources should be delivered directly to the providers of the service (e.g. nursery schools) through the channel of local authority grants, or to the users of the service (parents) in the form of credits or vouchers. There is much to be said for the latter. This report has repeatedly emphasised the leading role of the parents. He who pays the piper, calls the tune. If parents had 'nursery-credits', they could use their economic power, like other consumer groups, to ensure that the service met their needs and the needs of their children. But very careful study, followed by experimental pilot schemes, would be needed before any such general arrangements were introduced. It would be particularly important to ensure that a credit scheme did not generate its own expensive and bureaucratic administration. A credit scheme has the further advantage of providing a possible solution to the 'deadweight problem'. This term refers to the cost of providing a general, public and free benefit, where many people are already paying for it privately – as in the case of nursery education. With a credit scheme it is possible to recoup (in whole or part) the costs of public provision from the well-off through the tax system. See the *RSA Journal*, May 1993, for an elaboration of this approach. However, in this report there is no compromise with the principle of public provision of free pre-school education for all children.

A new solution

7.9   The arguments presented in the previous section of this chapter are not new. They are none the less cogent for that. However, there is an alternative – and rather more attractive solution to the problem. This develops Professor Sylva's (at first sight) paradoxical proposal of raising the age at which children begin 'compulsory' full-time schooling from five to six. Chapter 3 demonstrated that six is the normal age for the beginning of compulsory schooling throughout the world. In a few countries (notably in Scandinavia) the age is seven. In Europe, it is only the Netherlands, Ireland (de facto) and the UK that begin as early as five. It is not a coincidence that it is precisely those nations which start at five that are finding difficulty with the provision of systematic and high-quality pre-schooling. Hardly surprisingly, with the 'extra year' of full-time compulsory schooling, they *both* find it difficult to provide adequate resources for nursery education *and* have a poorly developed social recognition of the importance of early learning. Where full-time compulsory schooling is delayed to the age of six (or even seven), neither governments nor societies can easily overlook or neglect the case for pre-school education.

7.10   Part of that case is the argument developed throughout this report that pre-school early learning represents a distinct, essential and fundamental phase of education, without which it is difficult for children to progress successfully in school or into adult learning. While some of our children are helped through this foundation phase of learning in nursery schools and in homes with books and attentive adults, others are unprovided for. When the latter group enter primary education, they tend to be bewildered, discouraged and defeated by the challenge of formal learning. They are neither prepared nor ready for it. Such children are likely to become demotivated, drop-outs, or delinquent. They exact a heavy social cost in the longer term. And part of that cost is expressed in wasted educational investment. The UK is almost alone among the nations of the world in providing as many as eleven years of compulsory full-time education. The norm is ten; some countries (including highly successful ones, like Japan) manage with nine. There is little to show that we are making commensurate gains for this extra year of compulsory schooling. Explanations of this, relying on ideas of underperformance by our schools or even low intelligence of our children, seem implausible. It is more likely that the inadequate and inappropriate provision of early learning opportunities is having a detrimental effect on compulsory education.

7.11   How can one tell when children are ready for (full-time) school? In earlier times there was an idea that children who could touch their (left) ear by stretching their (right) hand over their head were ready for school. The age of five was chosen as the starting age for education in the Elementary Education Act (the Forster Act) of 1870. Until that time, most educational practice and the opinions of reformers favoured the age of six as the appropriate point for transfer from 'infant' to 'elementary' school. Robert Owen's infant school, established in 1816, provided half-time education for children aged two to six; Froebel also set the borderline at six: the Newcastle Report of 1861 drew the line at six, or even (in some places) seven. Until 1870, all the evidence suggested that the UK would adopt what has become common practice almost everywhere else in Europe, namely a starting age of six (or even seven). W.E.Forster, who was the draughtsman of the Bill, seems not to have attached much importance to the issue until the Bill was before Parliament. Members were divided in their support for five or six. Forster himself said that 'after what he had heard, he should be in favour of six'. But Disraeli (leading the opposition party, but supporting the Bill) persuaded the House of Commons to avoid delay, with a result that the amendment in favour of six was withdrawn. Although the question was raised again in the Lords, the age of five was allowed to stand and was duly incorporated in the Act. It is important to remember that the Act also made provision for an upper age limit – at thirteen. School Boards were empowered to fix any appropriate ages within the range five to thirteen. In practice – and parliament was aware that this would happen – most School Boards enforced the lower limit of five, but set the upper limit significantly below thirteen (variously at ten, eleven or twelve). The reason for this was, of course, an economic one: the older children were required for employment in factories. In other words, Parliament settled on the age of five for the start of schooling in the context of a general expectation (confirmed by existing practice) that schooling would end at about eleven. The issue for the reformers was whether to provide for six, or only five, years of elementary education. It should not surprise us that they chose the former – and set a starting age of five.

7.12   This account draws heavily on a fascinating study on *The Origins of Full-Time Compulsory Education at Five* (Szreter, 1964, *The British Journal of Educational Studies* Volume XIII No 1). Two further points may be added. First, it is notable that the idea of part-time attendance for young children was hardly discussed at all. The reasons appear to be that full-time schooling was intended to protect children from premature employment in the factories – or delinquency in the streets; and that (as with the issue of the starting age) reformers were keen to increase 'the gross amount of education' received. Secondly, from time to time after 1870 the issue of the starting age re-emerged for discussion. For example, the Code of 1905 claimed that 'there was reason to believe that attendance of children under five was often dangerous to health, and that there was also a mass of evidence pointing to the conclusion that a child who did not attend school before the age of six, compared favourably at a later stage with a child whose attendance had begun at an earlier age'. The question was considered again in 1908, 1918 and 1933, but nothing was done. It is time to reconsider it. Szreter recognised 'a vicious circle: the virtual absence of State provision of nursery education does harm to children in the first year of full-time infant education, while the fact that this year begins at the age of five-minus hinders the expansion of nursery education. If the resources at present tied up in the full-time schooling of five-year-old children were partially released for providing part-time education up to the age of six, a very considerable amount of it would become available.' (*The Origins of Full-Time Compulsory Education at Five*, Szreter, 1964, *The British Journal of Educational Studies* Volume XIII No 1). Szreter's proposal is the solution recommended here.

7.13   In their simplest form, the funding implications of the new solution involve the redistribution of one-eleventh of the budget for compulsory schooling (at present spent on the full-time primary education of five-year-olds) to enhance existing pre-school provision so as to provide three years of (half-time) high-quality early learning for all children aged three to five inclusive. The recurrent budget for primary and secondary education (in England) is of the order of £15 billion (1993-4). This figure includes Sixth Form and special provision. With an allowance for the fact that primary education tends to be funded less generously than secondary education, and to have larger classes – contrary to the practice recommended in this report – it is possible to estimate a 'notional saving' of the order of £1 billion, if the school starting age were raised to six. This is more than enough to cover the required recurrent sum estimated in paragraph 7.5 above, but not enough to provide for the three years of half-time nursery learning (three to five inclusive) which is envisaged and recommended here. One way of looking at the figures is to assume that half of the notionally released £1 billion would still be required for the half-day education of children aged five. This would yield a sum of about £500 million towards the required £600-£900 million set out in paragraph 7.5. The strategy of gradually tilting existing resources in favour of early learning could provide the rest. What is clear is that the combination of the arguments underlying the new solution, the idea of rebalancing of the educational budget, and the strong case for new investment in early learning, provides a firm reply to those who doubt whether we can afford it, or find acceptable ways of paying for it.

7.14   If the new solution were adopted, should the part-time foundation phase of early learning (between three and five inclusive) be compulsory? It would be logical to think so. The arguments presented throughout this report to emphasise the importance of good early learning lead naturally to a conclusion that the community should insist, not only that it be made available to all children, but also that they should be required to attend. But, as far as is known, no other country requires attendance at centre-based learning from the age of three. It is interesting to note that the Forster Act of 1870 did not require attendance, either. Compulsion was not introduced until 1876. Under existing legislation the form of compulsion for education between five and sixteen is noteworthy. The 1944 Education Act lays a responsibility on parents to ensure that their children receive an adequate education – either at home or in school. Section 36 makes clear that it is the duty of parents to secure the education of their children: 'it shall be the duty of the parent of every child of compulsory school age to cause him to receive efficient full-time education suitable to his age, ability and aptitude, either by regular attendance at school or otherwise'. An appropriate form of these words might also be used for the 'foundation phase' between three and six, as envisaged in the new solution. This would enable those parents who believed, and could demonstrate, that the home environment would provide a satisfactory context for early learning, to educate their children themselves, at least until six, while at the same time creating a general social understanding that half-time centre-based learning is normally appropriate from three to five inclusive. It would be important to apply the formula of the 1944 Education Act in a way that avoided the creation of a cumbersome bureaucracy of inspection and compulsion. At least in the first instance, it might be sensible to retain compulsion from the age of five, and to defer its introduction at earlier ages until the appropriate general social understanding had developed. The Newcastle Report of 1861 stated that 'what the State compels, it must also enable men to do'. This is a sound principle for government. If part-time education were compulsory (as defined above) for three to five year olds, there would be a much greater likelihood that it would be adequately resourced. Compulsion is probably the key to provision. However, no country at present makes pre-school education compulsory, even in the terms indicated above. Nonetheless, it is a view taken in this report that the question of compulsion should be publicly debated, since the logic of the argument leads so clearly in this direction.

7.15   Not all the members of the project's Advisory Committee are persuaded that the advantages of the new solution outweigh its disadvantages. What are the objections? Apart from inertia and the (false) assumption that the *status quo* must be right because it is there, there appear to be three major difficulties. The Department for Education is likely to be dismayed at what might be seen as a threat to the National Curriculum. This fear would be misplaced, since the arguments outlined above suggest that if the beginning of 'Key Stage 1' was deferred until the age of six – provided good early learning was available between three and five (inclusive) – the performance of children in compulsory full-time education would improve. The evidence of what is achieved in other countries (see Chapter 3) is pertinent. Secondly, practitioners and professionals tend to have a vested interest in the *status quo*. It will be important to persuade teachers and their representative organisations that the new solution offers a better deal for all concerned – children, parents and professionals. We must not allow the good to become the enemy of the best. Teachers, in particular, must be urged not to let the good things in the existing pattern of provision stand in the way of a better dispensation. Thirdly, parents may take a short-sighted view and seek to defend full-time and free primary education for five-year-olds, rather than welcome the provision of free part-time early learning for children from three to five inclusive, set in a context of extended day-care for those who wish it and are prepared to pay for it (on a means-tested basis). Probably, no single one of these objections by itself could prevent reform: but any two could. So it will be necessary for those who seek to pursue the new solution to form a strong alliance with at least two (and, if possible, all three) groups – parents, professionals, government. It is to be hoped that employers and the world of employment will play a leading role in the public debate of these issues. At the local level the attitude of Training and Enterprise Councils will be significant. Nationally, organisations like the CBI and TUC could and should – offer a clear lead.

Responsibility

7.16   Previous chapters have repeatedly identified the problems arising from the divisions of responsibility for early years provision. Two departments of central government (Health and Education) have statutory and moral responsibilities, and at least three others have associated interests (Employment, the Home Office and the Treasury). At the local level, responsibility is distributed between the Local Authorities and Training and Enterprise Councils, and (within local government) between social services and education departments. Divided responsibility rarely works well from the point of view of the client or user of services. *Divide et impera* was a Roman doctrine designed to serve the ruling power, not the ruled. Good government focuses responsibility and makes it accountable. This report has attempted to demonstrate that the provision of opportunities for good early learning for all our children is a collective social obligation. It is for Parliament to recognise this obligation and ensure that it is met. This will require new legislation. And it will be essential, if the outcome is to be satisfactory, to locate the central responsibility for implementation in one place. Since this report has consistently argued for the recognition of a 'seamless web' of learning and care, the logical alternatives appear to be the Department of Health, or the Department for Education or some new quasi-governmental agency designed on the model of the Manpower Services Commission. The first has a good record of responsible implementation following the passage of the Children Act of 1989. The second is the rational choice for a task that is primarily educational. There is much to be said for the third alternative, where there is a history of divided responsibility and lack of progress, and the need is urgent. But this would be, at best, a temporary measure. In the long run the responsibility for early education must lie with the Department for Education.

7.17   A similar problem exists at local level. Responsibility is at present divided between social services departments and Local Education Authorities. However, they are increasingly working together, partly as a result of local political initiatives, and partly because this is required under the Children Act 1989. In many authorities this is reflected in better communication between departments, but a number of authorities have adopted more radical solutions bringing together all services for young children into a single department. In addition to the direct provision of services, local authorities have important regulatory functions. However, since in recent years local government has in practice lost much of its independent power to raise revenue, it has to an extent moved from being a true level of government to becoming more like an agency of central government. This has inevitably led to questions about its future. The questions go beyond the matter of boundaries and the current review of local government. Some of them were set out in *Learning Pays* (RSA, 1991: 5.16-24). The problem was also considered by the National Commission, which recommended the creation of new locally accountable bodies to be known as Education and Training Boards (*Learning to Succeed*, Chapter 13). It is impossible at present to predict the outcome of the debate. This report agrees with the Commission that it is 'essential that there should continue to be an intermediate tier of locally accountable bodies between [central government] and individual schools', though these might well be regional – rather than local – bodies. When and if they come into existence, such bodies should be given the responsibility for the provision of ensuring that the statutory requirements are met in their own areas. Unless and until existing arrangements for local government are changed, this responsibility should rest with local authorities – which should seek to ensure that social services and education departments work in co-operation, with the latter taking the lead.

The timetable

7.18   The introduction of a new phase of education (for three- to five-year-olds, inclusive) cannot be achieved overnight or without careful preparation and training of staff. This is a major issue. There will be a serious shortfall of trained nursery teachers unless the new provision is introduced gradually. There is also an argument from established expectations which might suggest that the raising of the school starting age should not apply to children born before 1994. And sufficient time needs to be set aside for public debate. For all these reasons, it is proposed that 1999 should be chosen as the year for introducing the new solution; namely the raising of the school starting age to six and the creation of (first) an entitlement to (and later, perhaps, a requirement of attendance at) half-time pre-school education from three to five inclusive. This would allow a draft timetable, as follows:

1994-6   development of existing provision and preparation for the new solution (including a period for debate and consultation to achieve a consensus)

1997   introduction of an entitlement to early learning for all four-year-olds

1999   introduction of an entitlement (perhaps, a requirement?) for early learning for all children aged three to five inclusive; and deferral of the start of compulsory full-time schooling until the age of six.

Such a scheme allows children born in 1993 to have (at least) one year of pre-school; those born in 1994 to have (at least) two years of pre-school, before starting full-time schooling at age six in 2000; those born in 1995 to follow the same pattern as those born in 1994; and those born after 1995 to follow the new pattern of three years of pre-school followed by full-time schooling from the age of six. It is urged that as soon as possible (and not later than 1997) normal practice should allow *termly* admission to pre-school provision in the term following the relevant birthday of the child; or perhaps in the term in which the birthday falls.

7.19   During the transitional period (1994-8) it will be important to make steady progress towards the objectives. Local Authorities should be encouraged to make use of all forms of existing provision which satisfy (or can be helped to satisfy) appropriate standards of quality. We shall need to harness the existing diverse pattern of provision, public and private, playgroups and nursery schools, reception and nursery classes. But, as the National Commission argues: 'the ideal would seem to be an expansion of nursery education based on nursery schools and nursery classes in primary schools' (*Learning to Succeed*, p. 131). During this period Local Authorities may need to — and should be permitted to — charge fees on a means-tested basis, not only for the extended daycare element of the provision, but even — if necessary — for the half-day pre-school provision. Intelligent compromise should be encouraged, provided that there is no compromise on the issue of high quality and provided that the objective of a free provision for all children by 1999 is kept clearly in view. The cynical objection to the adoption of intelligent compromises in the transitional period — indeed, to the new solution as a whole — is that governments rarely honour long-term social 'deals' involving the redistribution of public funds. This is not borne out by experience. Nor is it wise in a free democracy to assume that good government is beyond our reach.

Conclusions

7.20   This chapter which has sought to identify a practical programme of action enabling us to realise the vision of a right start for all our children, leads to the following *conclusions*:

a) the Government has appeared to believe that the evidence of research has not yet demonstrated the value of good early learning: it is wrong to do so;

b) the Government has appeared to believe that the existing pattern of provision in the UK provides 'the best start in life' for every child: it is wrong to do so;

c) the underlying problem is one of finance — i.e. implicit national priorities;

d) other bodies need to pursue the issues of paid parental leave and the care of the pre-school children of those in employment;

e) more work is needed on the issue of the education and support of parents;

f) what is required is a statutory responsibility to provide free high-quality, half-day early learning for all children from the age of three in an integrated context of extended day care;

g) such a programme would cost a sum estimated at between £600 and £900 million p.a.;

h) the arguments from investment, priorities and relative value each lend support to the provision of substantial new funding for pre-school education;

i) a substantial contribution to the solution of the problem could be found by raising the age at which children begin compulsory full-time schooling from five to six;

j) this change would have a number of advantages:

    i. it would encourage a wider social recognition of the importance of early learning;

    ii. it would permit the identification of early learning as a distinct, essential and fundamental phase of education;

    iii. it would bring the UK into line with normal practice in most other countries;

    iv. it would have the potential to improve the performance of compulsory education from 6-16;

    v. it would enable the government to re-allocate funding to provide part-time pre-school education for children aged three to five inclusive, without requiring substantial new funds;

k) if this approach is adopted, consideration should be given to whether pre-school education should be compulsory (in the terms of the 1944 Education Act);

l) parents, professionals and the Government would each need to be persuaded of the wisdom of this approach;

m) it is essential to locate the responsibility for early learning in one place: for the time being there are good reasons for creating a special Commission to undertake the task;

n) the responsibility for ensuring that the statutory requirements are given local implementation should lie with local education and social services departments – and, in the event of local government reform, with their successors;

o) there needs to be a gradual, phased introduction of the new arrangements for three to six education;

p) during the transitional period it will be sensible and appropriate to build on existing provision wherever possible, provided that high quality provision is assured and the objective of a free provision for all children by 1999 is kept clearly in view.

7.21   Accordingly it is *recommended* that:

11   **the RSA and other bodies should pursue the issues of:**
    a) the education and support of parents
    b) paid parental leave
    c) the care of pre-school children of those in employment;

12   **the Government should immediately prepare legislation to create by 1999 a statutory responsibility for the provision of free, high-quality, half-day pre-school education for all children from the age of three, in an integrated context of extended day-care;**

13   **the Department for Education should give consideration to raising the age at which children begin compulsory full-time schooling from five to six, and transferring the resources released thereby to enable pre-school education (as defined in recommendation 12) to be made available for all children aged three to five inclusive;**

14 there should be a public debate of whether pre-school education should be made compulsory;

15 in order to ensure that the responsibility for early learning is clearly located in one place, a special Commission should be created to oversee the transition from the status quo;

16 Local Education Authorities should take responsibility for local provision;

17 the new arrangements should be introduced gradually by means of a carefully phased transition between 1994 and 1999.

8. Findings and Recommendations

'Upon the education of this country the fate of this country depends'

(Benjamin Disraeli, 1874)

> This chapter summarises the conclusions of the report. The RSA project posed three questions: does early learning matter? what is the nature of good practice? how can a universal entitlement to good early learning be provided? The answers are given. In particular, five major findings emerge: early learning is a distinct and fundamental phase of education; parents, professionals and the community as a whole form a 'triangle of care' and need to work in partnership; the quality of early learning provision is of over-riding importance; the resource constraints on provision can be overcome; to fail to do so would be condoning a national scandal. The report concludes by asking 'who is to do what by when?' and addressing its seventeen recommendations to those who are responsible for action.

Issues

8.1   Does early learning matter? This was the first and fundamental question which stimulated the RSA enquiry. The evaluation of the importance of early learning is the key issue. The study has found that pre-school education leads to immediate, measurable gains in educational and social development and lasting cognitive and social benefits in children – provided it is of high quality. While all children benefit, the impact of early education is strongest in children from disadvantaged backgrounds. The most important learning in pre-school education has to do with aspiration, motivation, socialisation and self-esteem. Good early learning encourages and develops 'mastery', without which successful schooling and adult learning is unlikely. Investment in high-quality and effective early education provides a worthwhile social and economic return to society in both developing and developed countries. As a consequence, there has been a rapid expansion in pre-school education during the last thirty years throughout the world, especially in developed countries – and most notably in Europe; this process appears set to continue.

8.2   What is the nature of good practice? This was the second major question. The report has repeatedly emphasised the critical importance of high quality provision – defined in terms of (a) a curriculum based on the principle of active learning and 'purposeful play', (b) the selection, training, retention and ratio of staff, (c) parental involvement, (d) buildings and equipment, (e) diversity of the peer group. As a consequence of (a), early entry to primary education and to Key Stage 1 of the National Curriculum is not a suitable alternative to high-quality pre-school education. Active and responsible learning is the key to the success of the most successful programmes. Nations where compulsory state education begins at the age of six (or even seven) are readier to recognise the importance of early learning, and to make provision for it, than those countries where it begins at five. Britain, together with Ireland and the Netherlands, is out of step with developments in the remainder of the European Union. International comparisons confirm that the salient features of good practice in the direction and management of the provision of early learning include:

* the integration of education and care;
* unified responsibility for provision;
* targets for growth by a specified year;
* coherent and thorough training of early years teachers and support staff;
* a curriculum based on the principle of 'purposeful play';
* effective linkage between the home and pre-school, and smooth progression between pre-school and primary school;
* adequate resources.

8.3   Children are most likely to thrive (and learn) in a secure triangle of care provided by parents, professionals and the community as a whole. But the role of parents is the most important for the welfare of the child. Parents should be thought of – and should learn to think of themselves – as aspiring to competence in a role which requires preparation, study and reflection, like any form of demanding work. For parents are their children's first and most important educators; and, like all good teachers, should strive to be 'warm demanders'. Confidence is an important quality in successful parenting, but parents need help in developing and sustaining confidence. What is needed is a real partnership between parents and professionals. The quality of early learning depends on a set of principles, not a favoured type of provision. The twelve principles fundamental to good practice yield a list of ten common features which should serve as guidelines for good early learning in group settings, or in the home. These principles and guidelines are already well established and widely recognised as the components of good practice. In particular, the quality of early learning depends on the quality of teachers and carers, the curriculum, and the role of parents. There is a professional continuum stretching from parents on one side to graduate (early years) teachers on the other; and training and professional development of high quality needs to be available at each stage. The professional teacher needs to acquire the practical skills of teaching, a theoretical understanding of learning (within and across subjects), and secure professional values. But early years teachers require a double competence: the ability to interpret the complexities of (for example) science or language in a form accessible to young children, and the mastery of a theory of learning development which they can apply to the diversity of children in their care. The diverse pattern of provision in the UK lacks adequate arrangements for quality review and quality assurance. For these and other reasons, there is a need for a clear national lead and a new legislative framework, backed up with appropriate funding, to ensure that all children are provided with opportunities for good pre-school education, and that parents are able to make well-informed choices.

8.4   What is the strategy for change? This was the third basic question. How can a universal entitlement to good early learning be provided? The review of the diverse pattern of provision in the UK concluded that it lacks coherence, co-ordination or direction. It fails to meet the needs of either children or parents; and it is unevenly and inequitably distributed. It also falls short in a number of ways of providing an assurance of high quality – without which the benefits of pre-school education are seriously diminished. Moreover, many of those most in need, and most likely to benefit, miss out. Both the (quantitative) statistical base and the (qualitative) knowledge base are inadequate and incomplete. The division of responsibility between the Health and Education Departments is a major difficulty – and so is the failure to grasp the principle of the integration of childcare and early learning. The Department for Education has neglected its moral responsibilities for supervising, registering, inspecting and ensuring the quality of pre-school education; and has failed to seek and obtain appropriate statutory authority. The Government has failed over many years to establish a national frame-work within which local developments could take place. While funding appears to be the major impediment to progress, in reality the problem is one of priorities. Pre-school education should be among a nation's first priorities. Ministers have offered an unconvincing and inadequate defence of the status quo, by setting a high value on diversity (at the expense of quality, effectiveness and choice), by expressing doubt about the value of pre-school education (in the teeth of the evidence of research and the experience of other countries), and by trusting in the private sector (without ensuring both that those most in need – and most likely to benefit – will thereby be provided for) and that the provision will be of statutory quality.

8.5   The Government has appeared to believe that the evidence of research has not yet demonstrated the value of good early learning: it is wrong to do so. The Government has appeared to believe that the existing pattern of provision in the UK provides 'the best start in life' for every child: it is wrong to do so. In fact, the underlying problem is one of finance – i.e. implicit national priorities. While other bodies need to pursue the issues of paid parental leave and the care of the children of those in employment, and more work is also needed on the issue of the education and support of parents, what is now required is a statutory responsibility to provide free high-quality, half-day early learning for all children from the age of three in an integrated context of extended day care. Such a programme would cost a sum estimated at between £600 and £900 million p.a.. While the arguments from investment, priorities and relative value each lend support to the provision of substantial new funding for pre-school education, a significant contribution to the solution of the problem could be found by raising the age at which children begin compulsory full-time schooling from five to six. This change would have a number of advantages:

* it would encourage a wider social recognition of the importance of early learning;
* it would permit the identification of early learning as a distinct, essential and fundamental phase of education;
* it would bring the UK into line with normal practice in most other countries;
* it would leave the potential to improve the performance of compulsory education from 6-16;
* it would enable the government to reallocate funding to provide part-time pre-school education for children aged three to five inclusive, without requiring substantial new funds.

If this approach is adopted, consideration should be given to whether pre-school education should be compulsory (in the terms of the 1944 Education Act). But parents, professionals and the Government will each need to be persuaded of the wisdom of this approach. It is essential to locate the responsibility for early learning in one place: there are good reasons for creating a special commission to undertake the task for the time being. The responsibility for ensuring that the statutory requirements are given local implementation should lie with Local Education Authorities, working in co-operation with social services departments (social work departments in Scotland) – and, in the event of local government reform with their successors. There needs to be a gradual, phased introduction of the new arrangements for the education of three- to six-year-olds. And during the transitional period it will be sensible and appropriate to build on existing provision wherever possible, provided that high quality provision is assured and the objective of a free provision for all children by 1999 is kept clearly in view.

Findings

8.6   From the review of the issues arising from a study of the importance of early learning, the nature of good practice and the search for a strategy of change, there arise five major findings. The first is the recognition that children's early learning, typically associated with the years three to six, forms a distinct and fundamental phase of education. It is not an 'optional extra', but a necessary foundation for successful schooling and adult learning. It has its own proper curriculum – which is distinct from, and preparatory to, Key Stage 1 of the National Curriculum. Those nations (like the UK) which have constructed a system of public provision for education which conceals or neglects this early learning phase have created a defective public understanding of the nature of good educational development. Good houses require strong foundations. A well-educated society needs nursery schools.

8.7   The second major finding is the importance of the triangle of care. There is a threefold responsibility for ensuring that every child enjoys a secure, warm and stimulating childhood. Parents, professionals and the community as a whole must work together in partnership since no one of them can be fully effective on their own. While each of these partners has their own proper role, they share a common purpose. Just as the medical profession in all its diversity is united in its aim to 'cure sometimes, relieve often, comfort always' – so the partners in the triangle of care need to come together in a common purpose to 'restrain sometimes, encourage often, love always'.

8.8   The third finding relates to quality. Both the evidence of research and the experience of other countries confirm the over-riding importance of high-quality provision for early learning. The ten common features of good practice are already well established in the UK, but need to be systematically applied and guaranteed through new arrangements for quality assurance.

8.9   The fourth major finding is that it is indeed possible for the UK to ensure that 'no child born after the year 2000 should be deprived of opportunity and support for effective early learning'. The resources required can be found. What has been lacking up to now is political will. This report has sought to demonstrate that investment in good early learning provides a worthwhile economic return. It has also argued that pre-school education should be recognised as a national priority. And it has suggested that even within a fixed educational budget, the relative value of nursery education is such as to justify a rebalancing of resources in favour of early learning. But the new approach outlined in Chapter 7 offers a way forward which is not only educationally attractive and cost effective in itself, but also designed to persuade even those who are unmoved by the arguments from investment, priorities or relative value. In such circumstances failure to make progress now would be a national disgrace.

8.10   And the fifth finding of this report is that in any event the current situation is little short of a national scandal. We have neglected the needs of the most vulnerable members of society – young children (especially those from deprived or disadvantaged backgrounds). Twenty-two years ago Margaret Thatcher saw what was required and published a White Paper which accepted the principle of nursery education. Governments of both the left and the right have subsequently abandoned the principle. For nearly a generation large numbers of the nation's children have been deprived of the right start to their lives, and society has paid the price in terms of educational failure and waste, low skills, disaffection and delinquency. Although remedial education for young people and adults can mitigate the damage, nothing can be done to retrieve the lost benefits of good early learning either for those who have missed it, or for the society which has neglected its responsibilities and wilfully overlooked the value and importance of providing all children with the right start. But we can do better in future.

Recommendations

8.11 Where does responsibility lie? Who should do what by when?. It is fatally easy for parents, educators, employers and governments to indulge in a game of 'passing the parcel' of responsibility and blame, while nothing effective happens. This report is addressed severally to each of these constituencies, as well as to others. While co-operation and agreement between the many interested parties will provide the best hope of success, this cannot be achieved without wise leadership. Consequently, the following recommendation is addressed to parliament and the bodies which can influence parliament:

parliament, political parties, parents, employers, the media, the churches and other voluntary, community and religious organisations should consider whether the provision for pre-school education in the UK is seriously inadequate, and take steps to persuade the Government to undertake an urgent review and act on its recommendations (recommendation 4, paragraph 4.21).

8.12 The role of education and those responsible for the education service, is also of the first importance in achieving reform and moving forward from where we are to where we need to be. Accordingly, the following recommendations are addressed to practitioners, professional bodies, and those responsible for (and engaged in) research, including the Department for Education, Local Education Authorities and OFSTED:

early years practitioners should draw up an authoritative Code of Conduct based on the principles and guidelines for good practice set out in this report (recommendation 9, paragraph 6.20);

professional bodies and institutions of training concerned with early childhood care and education should review their training and practice to ensure that they offer parents a real partnership (recommendation 7, paragraph 5.16);

those responsible for educational research develop a strategy for clarifying the nature and sequence of child development and 'mastery' learning to provide a theoretical framework for the training and sustaining of professional 'early years' teachers and carers (recommendation 2, paragraph 2.22);

the Government, trusts and universities make a substantial commitment to further quantitative and qualitative research into the impact of, and best practice in, the provision of early learning in order to test the conclusions of this report, and (where appropriate) to extend or qualify them (recommendation 1, paragraph 2.22).

8.13 But neither educators nor governments can easily bring about change without the consent and active support of the wider community. Persuasive arguments are not enough. Powerful alliances are also needed. Parents and employers, royal societies and community leaders, pressure groups and the press, must all work together to change the culture – by raising awareness of the importance of good early learning – change the law – to create a statutory and mandatory requirement for provision – and change the distribution of resources – to provide an assurance of good early learning for all. And so the following recommendations are addressed (inter alia) to the churches and religious leaders, and the RSA:

the churches, religious and community leaders should stimulate a major public debate on the subject of parenthood in order to establish exemplifications of good practice based on research and proven experience (recommendation 5, paragraph 5.16);

the RSA and other bodies should pursue the issues of:
a) the education and support of parents
b) paid parental leave
c) the care of pre-school children of those in employment (recommendation 11, paragraph 7.21);

the RSA should plan and organise a major international conference on 'good practice in pre-school education' to review and update the findings of this report in 1995 (recommendation 3, paragraph 3.19).

8.14 However, the majority of recommendations are addressed to the Government. The Government has the first responsibility and major powers. It can legislate, regulate, create funding initiatives, and seek to persuade. It needs to use all these powers to realise the vision set out in this report. Accordingly, the following recommendations are addressed to the Government:

the Government should consider how parents can be given access to systematic and appropriate education and support to enable them to fulfil their roles most effectively (recommendation 6, paragraph 5.16);

the Government should consider its position in relation to (a) paid parental leave, (b) the care of pre-school children of employed parents, and (c) pre-school education, and take steps to enable the community to fulfil its responsibility in each of these areas (recommendation 8, paragraph 5.16);

the Department for Education should review its plans for the professional development and training of early years teachers in the light of the claims made in this report, that -
a) the *curriculum* of early learning forms a fundamental, distinct and essential phase of education, without which it is difficult for children to progress successfully in school or into adult learning;
b) the double competence required of early years teachers – *especially* the mastery of an applicable theory of learning development – makes just as intense a professional demand on students as does the mastery of disciplines required of all teachers;
c) the training and development of early years teachers should be no less rigorous and demanding than that appropriate to any other teachers (recommendation 10, paragraph 6.20);

the Government should immediately prepare legislation to create by 1999 a statutory responsibility for the provision of free, high-quality, half-day pre-school education for all children from the age of three, in an integrated context of extended day-care (recommendation 12, paragraph 7.21);

the Department for Education should consider raising the age at which children begin compulsory full-time schooling from five to six, and transferring the resources released thereby to enable pre-school education (as defined in recommendation 12) to be made available for all children aged three to five inclusive (recommendation 13, paragraph 7.21);

there should be a public debate of whether pre-school education should be made compulsory (recommendation 14, paragraph 7.21);

in order to ensure that the responsibility for early learning is clearly located in one place, a special Commission should be created to oversee the transition from the *status quo* (recommendation 15, paragraph 7.21);

Local Education Authorities should take responsibility for local provision (recommendation 16, paragraph 7.21);

the new arrangements should be introduced gradually by means of a carefully phased transition between 1994 and 1999 (recommendation 17, paragraph 7.21).

8.15   None of these things will happen without an assertion of political will, accompanied by popular support and directed through decisive leadership. The translation of national aspirations into reality cannot be achieved by government alone. It requires the co-operation, effort and enterprise of many agencies and all parts of society. Political will inevitably reflects the general will of society. But political leadership can shape the general will. Progress is possible. Nations have learned to free slaves, end child labour, extend the franchise to women. We can decide to stop neglecting the early education of our children. We may expect a range of economic, social and personal benefits if we do so. But these are not the most compelling reasons for action. We should act because it is *right*. Our children's children will not readily forgive us, if we decline to face the challenge, or fail.

APPENDIX A

Members of the Project's Advisory Committee

The project was supported by an Advisory Committee under the guidance of the RSA Education Advisory Group. Sole responsibility for the substance and text of the report lies with the author.

Sir Christopher Ball (Chairman) *Director of Learning, RSA, Project Co-Director*

Professor Kathy Sylva, *Department of Child Development, University of London, Project Co-Director*

Lesley James, (Secretary) *Education Projects Manager, RSA*

Lesley Abbott, *Principal Lecturer, Early Years, The Manchester Metropolitan University*

Catherine Baines, *Community Services Division, Department of Health*

Liz Bavidge, *Executive Committee, Women's National Commission*

Michael Brandon, *Partner, Korn/Ferry International*

Liz Cousins, *EBP Manager, Gloucestershire TEC*

Joanna Foster, *Chair, UK Council UN International Year of the Family*

Professor Philip Gammage, *Institute of Education, University of Nottingham*

Brenda Hancock, *Equal Opportunities Commission*

Kathleen Lund, *Group Director Education and Social Service, London Borough of Hillingdon*

Annette Holman, *Regional Adviser Pre 5s, Strathclyde Regional Council*

Margaret Lochrie, *Chief Executive Officer, Pre-School Playgroups Association*

Melian Mansfield, *Chair, Campaign for State Education*

Angie Mason, *BBC Select*

Margaret Murray, *Head of Education Policy Group, CBI*

Richard Osmond, *Director Group Personnel, The Post Office*

Alan Parker, *Education Officer, Association of Metropolitan Authorities*

Professor Christine Pascal, *Chair, Early Childhood Education, Worcester College of Higher Education*

Gillian Pugh, *Director of Early Childhood Unit, National Children's Bureau*

Iram Siraj-Blatchford, *Lecturer in Early Childhood Education, University of Warwick*

David Smith, *City Education Officer, Corporation of London*

Philippa Stobbs, *Council for Disabled Children*

Michael Taylor, *UK Director, The Save The Children Fund*

APPENDIX B

The responses

Summary of responses to the leaflet 'Start Right: the Importance of Early Learning

10,000 leaflets, reproduced on pages 81-82, were distributed in February 1993. They were sent to a wide variety of organisations including playgroups, schools, Training and Enterprise Councils, employers and groups with an interest in early learning. Replies were received from about 100 people. The overwhelming majority came from professionals within education including a large number from headteachers of nursery and infant schools. Organisations directly involved in early learning, e.g. Pre-school Playgroups Associations, were also well represented. Despite mailing a broad cross-section of small, medium and large companies, the RSA received only a very small number of replies from employers. Six of the replies were from men, including one M.P.

I. The definition of early learning

No-one disputed the definition of early learning as stated in the leaflet.

2. National aims

Similarly, the RSA's vision of a 'learning society', in which everyone participates in education and training (learning) throughout their lives, was welcomed and applauded. The premise that 'central to this is the availability to everyone of good experiences of early learning' was widely endorsed and not questioned by any respondent.

3. The issues and some key questions

i. Importance

The importance of early learning was not questioned and research data was quoted in a significant number of responses. This research was invariably from the High/Scope and Head Start programmes carried out in the United States. The statistic that $1 spent on good early learning was saved many times over in 'compensatory' payments was often stated.

The educational benefits given as examples were more varied and included:

★ diagnosis of speech impairment or difficulties could be made at an earlier stage

★ fewer children were referred to educational psychologists.

A significant social benefit mentioned by several respondees was that gender and race issues could be tackled early and in a thoughtful and considered way.

ii. Good practice

Many people sent details of their early learning programmes, in some cases reflecting the importance placed on early learning by individual local authorities. What was significant was the plea, often made, for a 'standard of good practice' which would apply to all providers of early learning.

A recurring theme was the value of the 'team' approach to staffing in early learning centres. The point was often made that all members of the team were equally important; each had an individual role to play; all needed easy access to training and relevant qualifications; and the team must be led by a qualified teacher.

It was noted several times that good early learning does not come from a 'ghetto' of the children of the most disadvantaged families being concentrated in one school, which is often current practice.

START RIGHT

THE IMPORTANCE OF EARLY LEARNING

An RSA enquiry led by Sir Christopher Ball

RSA

The Royal Society for the encouragement of Arts, Manufactures & Commerce

JANUARY 1993

SPONSORS

The project is funded by
Esmée Fairbairn Charitable Trust
Bernard van Leer Foundation
London East TEC

Please send comments and advice on this project by the end of March 1993 to:

Sir Christopher Ball
Director of Learning
RSA
8 John Adam Street
London WC2N 6EZ
Tel: 071 930 5115
Fax: 071 839 5805

Your views matter. If you have firm opinions on the importance of early learning why not write to your MP also?

THE RSA – IDEAS ACROSS FRONTIERS

The RSA (Royal Society for the encouragement of Arts, Manufactures and Commerce) is an instrument of change: it works to create a civilised society based on a sustainable economy. It uses its independence and the resources of its Fellowship in the UK and overseas to stimulate discussion, develop ideas and encourage action.

Its main fields of interest today are business and industry, design and technology, education, the arts and the environment. Three themes underlie the Society's current involvement in these areas: *A Learning Society, A Sustainable World* and *Living and Working: future patterns.*

Start Right is the third major project to be launched under the theme 'A Learning Society'.

TARGETS

On the assumption that the project can reach a clear view on the importance of early learning, the nature of good practice and an effective strategy for change, it will seek to develop a shared national target that: no child born after the year 2000 (in the UK) should be deprived of opportunity and support for effective early learning. What else? What more?

THE CASE FOR THE PROJECT

'All I really need to know about how to live and what to do and how to be I learned in kindergarten.'
(Robert Fulghum)

'Can we afford not to give our children a good start in life?' *(Professor Kathy Sylva)*

'Effective systems of education must be developed bottom-up ... resources need to be tilted in favour of early learning.' *(Sir Christopher Ball)*

'Shall they all read?' *(A child's comment in the UN charter on the Rights of the child)*

'The government is determined that every child in this country should have the very best start in life'
(John Major)

PROJECT TEAM

Director Sir Christopher Ball *RSA Director of Learning*
Co-Director Professor Kathy Sylva *Department of Child Development and Primary Education, Institute of Education, University of London*
Project Manager Lesley James *RSA Education Secretary*

The project is supported by an Advisory Group under the guidance of the RSA Programme Committee.

EARLY LEARNING - WHAT IS IT?

By 'early learning' we mean the formal and informal learning of young people aged 0–7 - language and literacy, number and shape, co-ordination and self control, solving problems, understanding the needs of others, developing self esteem, trust, justice … The foundation for all future learning takes place in play-groups, with childminders, in nurseries and primary schools, on the street and through television, but most of all at home. Teachers are important. Parents are fundamental. A nation's future rests more and more on the quality of its children's early learning experiences.

NATIONAL AIMS

The RSA's vision is for a *learning society* in the UK in which everyone participates in education and training throughout their lives. It will support them as citizens, in their employment and their leisure.

A learning society should make provision *for all* to learn *through life*, at home, in school and college, and at work, achieving high standards at the pace, time and place that best suits them.

Central to this is the availability to everyone of good experiences of early learning.

But the translation of national aspirations into reality requires the co-operation, effort and enterprise of many individuals and organisations, and of the government. Will you help?

THE ISSUES AND SOME KEY QUESTIONS

1. IMPORTANCE

Does early learning matter?

If so, is its importance measurable in educational, social and economic terms?

Do the beneficial effects of good early learning last?

What are the experiences of other nations and societies?

2. GOOD PRACTICE

How can parents best contribute to their children's early learning?

What is the contribution of nursery schools, play-groups or child-minding?

What constitutes good practice in the early learning curriculum?

How can we advise and support teachers, carers and parents in their work and play with children?

How should government and the community give enduring support to the services which foster early learning?

3. A STRATEGY FOR CHANGE

If early learning matters:

How are we to provide a universal entitlement to good early learning in a learning society?

What is the relative effectiveness of legislation, resource-provision, persuasion?

What are the roles of parents, schools, LEAs, Social Services, TECs and LECs, employers, professional bodies, voluntary bodies, pressure groups, government?

Why is it that 'things widely and long asserted to be sensible and urgent do not happen'?

PROJECT OBJECTIVES

- To describe current provision for and participation in early learning in the UK and comparable nations

- to review and evaluate the evidence for the educational, social and economic value of early learning

- to identify barriers to participation for different social, regional and ethnic groups

- to define and disseminate kinds of good practice in early learning

- to develop an effective strategy for change such that opportunities for good early learning shall be available to all children in future

- and to make it happen.

(but NOT to reinvent the wheel – or to produce yet another worthy but ineffective report)

TIMING AND PROGRAMME OF WORK

1993	Consultation, forming new alliances, identifying impediments and resolving them; Research and review of responses to this leaflet;
early 1994	Report and recommendations;
1994	Regional meetings, confirming the alliance, preparing for change; The two Directors will work together to implement this programme, Professor Sylva taking the lead in conceptualisation and research, Sir Christopher Ball concentrating on alliances and strategies for change.

iii.   A strategy for change

There was a noticeable sense of frustration within many of the replies. Many stated that this project was following a rather 'well-worn path' which to date, had yielded little. The 'Rumbold Report' was frequently praised but the point was then made that it hadn't actually changed government provision or attitudes.

'Early learning' is available in a variety of forms, in a variety of settings. Many who responded felt that this multiplicity of providers had led to some unfortunate effects:

*   it was difficult to get a clear, unequivocal view of the current provision in the UK
*   the 'voice' of early years is fragmented, reflecting the diverse provision
*   parents found it extremely difficult to get a clear picture of what was available within their own areas
*   the 'purpose' of early learning is not always clear: is it educational, is it providing a place of safety for some children, is it childcare, is it compensatory?

A theme recurring strongly throughout the replies was the importance of parents. Their role as first educators was often made. The need for parents to be involved in the education system right from the beginning recurred frequently; as did the problem that many parents were not aware of the value of good early learning and therefore did not insist that it should be available for their children.

A number of the replies from nursery schools and similar centres gave examples of the workshops and courses which they ran for parents. These 'parenting skills' courses proved very popular with, and beneficial for, the parents and had 'knock-on' benefits for their children.

One reply gave a vivid example of parental power. A Local Authority had been persuaded to reverse its decision to close all of its nursery schools as a result of pressure from the parents in the area.

Several replies made the point that if children are to be treated equally, funding had to come from the public purse. Any other solution would merely reinforce the gulf which already exists in our society between the 'haves' and 'have nots'.

The need for equality within education was made frequently, and was particularly well made by one respondee: **'If all children are to be assessed at the age of 7, then all children should start the education race from the *same* point.'**

The Impact of Early Learning on Children's Later Development

Professor Kathy Sylva, *Institute of Education, University of London*

This review will examine the evidence which supports the widely held belief that early learning has lasting impact on the course of children's later lives. 'Early learning' is defined here as learning which occurs outside the home before school entry. To limit the scope even more, the review will concentrate on learning in centre-based settings in which 'education' is one of the expressed objectives. This includes learning which takes place in nursery schools and classes, day nurseries or childcare centres, and playgroups. Home care and child minders are excluded as their aim is primarily care.

State provision is evaluated in this review as well as voluntary (e.g. playgroups) and private education. The focus is on research from the United Kingdom and North America, although brief mention will be made of important studies from other countries.

Those sceptical about the need to invest in early education may be open to the idea that early development is important. Often they lack hard evidence about the impact of early learning or the ways in which its quality determines whether or not early education has lasting effects. Sometimes political scepticism stems simply from lack of information, combined with the fact that the chain of causality may be more than a decade long. Some scepticism lingers from early research that showed that the effects of pre-school experiences 'wash out' soon after school begins. Many policy makers in the 90s fail to question the scientific rigour of the research findings they cite. Sceptics may, for example, point to the studies in the 70s and 80s which showed that early educational programmes for disadvantaged children did not raise scores on IQ tests. Unfortunately, few are aware that the more rigorous research of the 80s and 90s has shown lasting benefits of pre-school education which are far more important than IQ scores. Results of the early studies have not been overturned, i.e. the IQ results were not proved wrong; we have discovered that the benefits of early learning appear in 'life skills', social and economic outcomes rather than in tests of formal intelligence.

Instead of diving head-first into the technicalities of research methods, the review will begin by examining research findings from individual studies, with comments on the relative strengths and weaknesses of each research design. It is hoped that this commentary will provide a 'painless tutorial' on research methods while presenting the findings of several decades of research.

Any rationale for investment in programmes of early learning must include answers to the different kinds of scepticism outlined in the opening paragraphs. Justification for investment must demonstrate the scientific grounds for high quality early learning. This review will examine the key studies and attempt to create a critical framework for evaluating their scientific rigour.

Research in the USA on pre-school programmes for disadvantaged children

The American project Head Start, a legacy of Lyndon Johnson's War on Poverty (Valentine, 1979) has received government funding for two decades in the hope that it would 'break the cycle of poverty'. A simple input/output model was used in early studies on the impact of Head Start. Typically, IQ or attainment test scores of pre-school 'graduates' were compared to scores of control children who had no pre-school experiences. Initial evaluations seriously underestimated the value of the programme (Campbell & Erlebacher, 1970; Smith & Bissell, 1970) by focusing on measures of intelligence as the main indicator of success. Sadly, they found that early IQ gains quickly 'washed out', leaving graduates of Head Start no different from control children.

I.I   **The recent Head Start meta-analysis**

More recent evaluations have employed sophisticated research methods and looked at a wider array of child outcomes. In 1985, a synthesis of research findings was published (McKey et al., 1985), which combined in a single meta-analysis the results of 210 studies evaluating the impact of Head Start. To enable comparison amongst the studies, findings were converted to statistical 'effect sizes' and comparisons were made across different sites, target groups, and tests on children.

McKey and his colleagues concluded that Head Start had immediate, positive effects on children's cognitive ability. Unfortunately, the cognitive gains were no longer apparent after the end of the second year at school (see Fig.1). Head Start also had short-term positive effects on children's self-esteem, scholastic achievement, motivation and social behaviour, but these advantages also disappeared by the end of the third year in school (see Fig.2). The authors of the meta-analysis point out that the studies were designed so differently and ranged so widely in terms of rigour that it was impossible to come to firm conclusions on many questions, including those concerning the impact of parental involvement. Most studies included in this synthesis of research did not control adequately for pre-intervention differences in children's ability, many studies were on one site only, and few used 'control' groups of comparable characteristics.

Figure 1.   *Immediate effects and long-term effects of Head Start on IQ, school readiness and achievement measures (treatment control studies). From McKey et al (1985)*

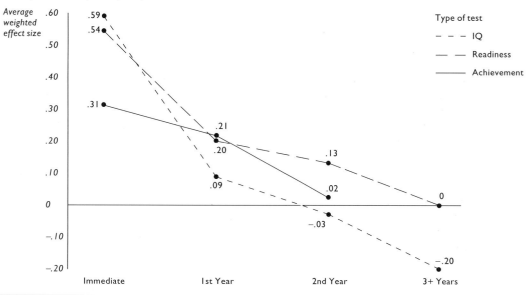

Figure 2.   *Immediate effects and long-term effects of Head Start on self-esteem, achievement motivation and social behaviour (treatment/ control and pre/post studies combined). From McKey et al (1985)*

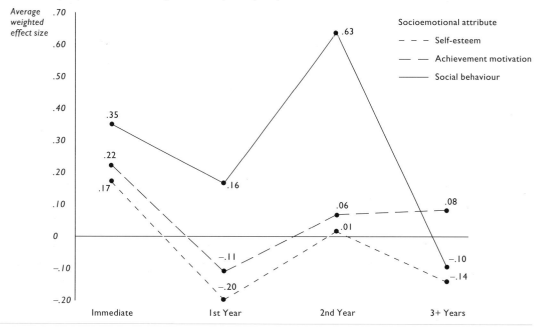

1.2   Smaller controlled studies on Head Start

The smaller, better controlled studies of the effects of Head Start have yielded more robust findings. A well designed study by Lee, Brooks-Gunn & Schnur (1988) compared the outcomes of 969 disadvantaged children who had experienced three different pre-school environments: Head Start, some other pre-school programme and no pre-school. Large, initial differences on a wide range of outcomes were found at school entry, with Head Start children lower on almost all measures. After adjusting for initial scores (because the Head Start sample was lower), Head Start children showed *larger gains* on measures of social and cognitive functioning ('readiness for school') compared to children in the other two groups. Head Start was effective in 'closing the gap' but did not succeed in doing so completely because its children began at greater levels of disadvantage.

Notable in Lee's study were the large gains made by Black children in Head Start. In many evaluative studies of pre-school it has been shown that 'pre-school intervention is particularly effective for the most economically disadvantaged children' (Zigler, 1987). Lee employed analysis of co-variance to disentangle the effects of race from those of initial test scores. They reported that Blacks gained more than Whites, even when controlling for initial levels of ability. Further, Black students of below average ability gained more than their counterparts of average ability. They concluded that their study demonstrates the effectiveness of Head Start: 'not only were those students most in need of pre-school experience likely to be in Head Start programs, but also that those Black students who exhibited the greatest cognitive disadvantage at the outset appeared to benefit most from Head Start participation' (p.219).

1.3   The effects of 'high quality' pre-school education programmes in the U.S.: further meta-analysis research

The failure to find a long-term impact of early education has not been confined to Head Start (see Porter, 1982, from Australia). However, there is cause for optimism when examining a programme of high quality. A group of American researchers carried out a meta-analysis of the effects of compensatory education on pre-school programmes which employed rigorous research designs. Lazar et al., (1982) limited their meta-analysis to pre-school projects with sample sizes greater than 100 children, which used norm-referenced assessment tests, comparison/control groups, and followed up children well beyond school entry. By these strict criteria eleven carefully monitored programmes were subjected to a statistical exercise which enables researchers to compare the size of effect across many different studies. The researchers located approximately 2000 pre-school "graduates" and their matched controls at the age of nineteen in order to document their educational and employment histories. In addition they interviewed the youths and their families.

Results from the eleven studies showed that attendance at excellent, cognitively oriented pre-school programmes was associated with later school competence. More specifically, pre-school graduates were less likely to be assigned to 'special' education or to be held back in a year-group while their peers moved up a grade. Interviews carried out at age 19 showed the nursery group to have higher aspirations for employment.

1.4   The High/Scope research

The most carefully controlled of the eleven programmes reviewed by Lazar was the Perry Pre-school Project, later known as High/Scope. This curriculum is of exceptionally high quality and it includes a complex training scheme for staff and sound parent participation. The programme has been subjected to careful evaluation for almost 30 years and has consistently shown striking results (Berrueta-Clement et al., 1984). Although an initial IQ advantage for pre-school graduates disappeared by secondary school, there were startling differences in other outcomes between the 65 children who attended the half-day educational programme over two years and the control group of 58 children who had remained at home. Table 1 summarises the results when children were 19 years of age.

Table 1   The long-term effects of pre-school education. From Berrueta-Clement et al (1984).

| | Group | | |
Outcome	Attended preschool	Did not attend preschool	p value
% Employed (n=121)	59	32	0.032
High school graduate (or its equivalent) (n=121)	67	49	0.034
%With college or vocational training (n=121)	38	21	0.029
% Ever detained or arrested (n=121)	31	51	0.022
Females only: teen pregnancies/100 (n=49)	64	117	0.084
Functional competence (APL survey: possible score 40) (n=109)	24.6	21.8	0.025
% of years in special education (n=112)	16	28	0.039

Results from further follow-up at age 27 appear in Figure 3. They are confirmed, especially with regard to delinquency, by Lally, Mangione and Honig (1988) who also found that preschool attendance lowered the rate of anti-social behaviour in adolescence.

Figure 3.   High/Scope Perry Preschool Study: Effects of the programme at age 27. From Schweinhart and Weikart (1993).

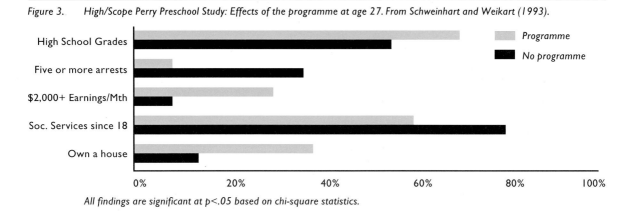

All findings are significant at p<.05 based on chi-square statistics.

Further analysis at age 27 showed:

* significantly higher percentage of car ownership (30% vs 13%)

* a significantly higher level of schooling completed (71% vs 54% completing 12th grade or higher)

* a significantly lower percentage receiving social services at some time in the past ten years (59% vs 80%)

* significantly fewer arrests by age 27 (7% vs 35% with 5 or more), including significantly fewer arrested for crimes of drug taking or dealing (7% vs 25%).

Schweinhart & Weikart (1993) reported a cost-benefit analysis which shows that for every $1000 that was invested in the pre-school programme, at least $7160 (after adjustment for inflation) has been, or will be, returned to society. These calculations were based on the financial cost to society of juvenile delinquency, remedial education, income support, and joblessness - set against the running costs of an excellent pre-school programme. The economic analysis also estimates the return to society of taxes from the higher paid pre-school graduates.

There have been two other cost benefit analyses carried out on pre-school interventions, both in the US. Barnett and Escobar (1990) presented data from a pre-school language intervention curriculum studied by Weiss (1981) and a comprehensive early daycare programme for disadvantaged families studied by Seitz, Rosenbaum and Apfel (1985). Both studies showed that the costs of the programmes were more than offset by the savings later on in the children's schooling and medical care.

Although American studies cannot prove that *all* pre-school programmes will bring lasting benefits, they demonstrate that early education can change the course of children's lives, especially those from disadvantaged backgrounds. It is interesting to note that most successful programmes involved some element of parent involvement (Woodhead, 1989; Lazar and Darlington, 1982). The evaluation research studies reviewed here are the most powerful justification for pre-school education because their research designs were rigorous, often employed experimental methods with random assignment to 'educational experiences'. Furthermore, studies reviewed in Section 1.3 and 1.4 employed a wide range of outcome measures and collected information on children up to and including adulthood. Although the samples are usually small, the experimental designs and longitudinal data collection allow the researchers to make strong claims that the pre-school experiences actually *caused* lasting cost-effective outcomes.

It is clear that some, but certainly not all, pre-school experiences put children on the path to greater school commitment, better jobs and lower rates of anti-social behaviour. With another cohort of children, Weikart and his colleagues compared the effects of three different curricula (Schweinhart, Weikart & Larner, 1986). They found that children from the High/Scope programme, a 'free play' programme and also a formal pre-school curriculum all had increased IQs at school entry. However, follow-up at the age of 15 showed that children who had attended the formal programme engaged more in anti-social behaviour and had lower commitment to school than those who attended the two programmes based on play. Thus, raised IQ at school entry does not necessarily give children a right start to school success. Only the children who experienced active learning programmes before school retained the advantage of their early education, an advantage they showed by pro-social behaviour and higher confidence in adolescence.

British research on the effects of pre-school attendance

2   The British research mirrors that for the U.S. with interventions during the 1970s aimed at 'closing the poverty gap' leading to disappointment (Smith & James, 1977) when the initial gains tended to 'wash out'. Many short-term studies found that pre-school attendance was associated with improved performance, eg., Turner (1977) found that children attending playgroups had higher language scores six months after initial testing compared to children at home.

2.1   **Controlled comparative studies**

The next study to be reviewed is one conducted by Jowett and Sylva (1986) in Britain. This is a quasi-experimental study which compared two groups of children entering the reception class, one coming from state nursery classes and the other from voluntary playgroups. There were 45 children in each group and all came from working-class backgrounds. It is a 'quasi-experiment' in that many background variables which might distinguish the two groups of children were carefully controlled. The children were matched on family structure, age, sex, and parental occupation since British and American studies show that different kinds of families use different kinds of services. In this study, 'parent choice' was controlled to some extent because children were drawn from neighbourhoods where there was only one form of half-day education: *either* playgroup or state nursery.

Jowett and Sylva found that the children who had attended LEA nursery engaged in more purposeful and complex activity in the reception class than did the children who attended playgroup; they chose more 'demanding' educational activities. Nursery children were more likely than the playgroup children to initiate contacts with the teacher that were "learning orientated" while the playgroup children approached teachers for help. Table 2 presents important findings on independence; the nursery graduates were more persistent and independent when they encountered obstacles (p<.01) in their school work or play. This study shows that the *kind* of pre-school education a child experiences affects the ease with which she begins her school career.

Table 2.   *Reactions to children's task difficulty, from Jowett and Sylva (1986).*

Term	Group	Asks for help %	Gives up %	Persists %
Autumn	Nursery N=78	17	1	82
	Playgroup N=77	36	22	42
Summer	Nursery N=63	14	17	68
	Playgroup N=37	49	30	22

2.2   **The impact of pre-school education on children's SAT performance (Standard Assessment Tasks)**

There have been two studies of the effect of early learning at pre-school on children's educational assessment at the age of seven. The National Foundation for Educational Research Consortium (1992) carried out a large national survey and found children who attended 'nursery' (many kinds of provision) did no better than those who did not. However, a more tightly controlled study, carried out by Shorrocks et al., (1992), found that 'nursery' attendance led to better performance in English, Science and Mathematics. This second study controlled statistically for the effect of family background, which was not done in the NFER research, because it is well known that poorer children are more likely to get a place at nursery.

2.3   **The Child Health and Education Study (CHES) on a birth cohort**

A longitudinal study by Osborn and Milbank (1987) on approximately 8,400 children born in 1970 showed a clear association between pre-school attendance and educational outcomes (reading, maths) and social ones (behaviour problems) at the age of ten. The authors claim that pre-school attendance *brought about* the greater cognitive performance of its graduates. But is the evidence firm? 'Birth cohort' studies such as this do not randomly assign children to different pre-school experiences. Instead the researchers follow a large group of children through childhood and document what happens to them. Some attended day nurseries, some nursery schools or classes, some went to voluntary playgroups and a few stayed at home with their families until school age. Altogether, the children who attended an educationally oriented pre-school had better cognitive and social functioning at the end of primary school than those who remained at home or attended a care-oriented centre.

Figure 4 shows that the most disadvantaged children were more likely to receive pre-school provision and moreover were much more likely to be in the maintained sector.

Figure 4.   *Pre-school experience by Social Index group, from Osborn and Milbank (1987)*

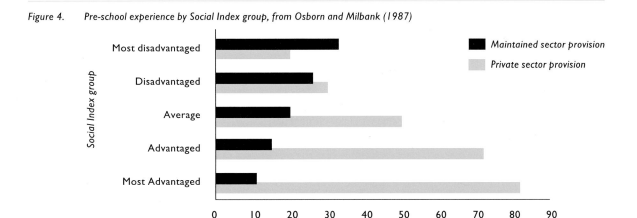

The authors put into rank order the kinds of pre-school experiences which are associated with the best outcomes. These are: private playgroups, community playgroups, nursery schools. Nursery classes, home care (no pre-school experience at all), and day nurseries were associated with poorer results. Did playgroups *cause* good outcomes and day nurseries bad? We know that children from the most disadvantaged homes attend day nurseries and also playgroups cater for, in the main, a middle class clientele. Although the researchers attempted to control for different intake by statistical adjustment based on social indicators such as family income, it seems doubtful that complete adjustment could be made. In the 80s we have learned to use baseline data to see the 'value added' by various educational experiences. In the absence of this, the CHES researchers tried to control *post hoc* for different characteristics of children who ended up in different kinds of provision. They found that the kinds of pre-schools which performed 'better' in terms of outcome are the very same ones which cater for more privileged children. It is impossible to draw firm causal conclusions from studies which control for intake using post-hoc statistics in the absence of rigorous control.

2.4   Professor Clark's review of British research on the effects of pre-school attendance

In 1988, Margaret Clark published an extensive review funded by the Department of Education and Science on the evidence concerning the effects of pre-school provision. First she rated the kinds of provision children attended and found that the largest provider of early learning 'places' in the UK is the playgroup movement; this was also noted by Bruner (1980) and Brophy, Statham and Moss (1992). She reviewed all the major British research studies on enrolment, characteristics of provision, curriculum, special needs, continuity with school, and a host of other topics. Her extensive review covered small scale studies as well as large ones but it led to few firm conclusions. She said that:

a)   most studies showed that attendance at pre-school of some kind was associated with positive benefits for the children;

b)   British research did not show benefits lasting beyond the infant school;

c)   there was insufficient research to demonstrate which kind of provision brought about the most successful outcomes.

d)   Lastly, she called for more research to discover which children benefitted/needed the different types of provision.

Learning in daycare

3   In daycare, education and care are combined in a single setting.

3.I   **The effects of daycare on children's emotional development**

Most research studies have looked at the effects of daycare on children's emotional adjustment, especially their attachment to their mothers (Clarke-Stewart, 1989., Kagan, Kearsley & Zelazo, 1978). There is still disagreement amongst scholars as to whether early entrance into daycare, say before the age of one year, is detrimental to children's later development. Studies in Sweden by Andersson (1989) and Gunarsson (1985) have followed children until entry at secondary school and have found no evidence that daycare for very young children harms their social or emotional development. On the other hand, studies in the U.S. by Moore (1975), Goldberg & Esterbrooks (1988), and Vandell and Corasaniti (1990) all found that early entry into daycare was associated with anxious attachments to the mother, emotional dependence and poor relationships with peers, including aggression. Reconciliation of such conflicting results will require discussion of quality in childcare as well as age of entry.

Families choose childcare for pressing economic and social reasons. Some research studies indicate that the outcome for children who attend *full-time* daycare, especially for children under one year, is far from satisfactory. Unfortunately, many of the children attend low quality centres and very careful research is needed to tease apart the effect of quality from age of entry and hours of attendance. After reviewing the research, Sylva (1992 a) concluded that high quality daycare leads to positive outcomes and low quality to adverse ones. We will now concentrate on the effects of early learning in daycare for children who enter after the first birthday.

3.2   **CHES study on daycare effects**

Osborn and Milbank (1987) studied thousands of children born in 1972, some of whom spent their early years in daycare centres run by the local authorities in Britain. The researchers compared the educational and social outcomes of children who had attended full-time daycare with those who had gone either to half-day 'educational' programmes or remained at home. They found that the daycare group had lower maths scores and higher incidence of behaviour problems during primary school. Why?

The answer probably lies partly in which families managed to obtain one of the scarce places in local authority daycare. McGuire and Richman (1986) found that children attending daycare centres run by Social Services Departments had ten times more behaviour and emotional problems as children in the same authority attending playgroups. Furthermore, the children in daycare were difficult to manage and they came from families with multiple problems requiring a great deal of emotional support from the staff and help with child rearing.

There are other problems in local authority daycare in the UK. A recent study by Sylva, Siraj-Blatchford and Johnson (1992) found that staff in the social service sector nurseries had too little knowledge of the National Curriculum to lay a firm foundation for it during the pre-school years. In contrast, teachers in the education sector were well informed about the National Curriculum pertaining to primary children and devised nursery school programmes based on assessing the educational needs of children and fostering learning tailored to individuals.

3.3   **Comparison with other countries**

We turn now to daycare in other countries to continue our search for the long-term consequences of both excellent and poor quality pre-school programmes.

Research from Sweden tells a very different story; instead of leading to educational and social problems, Andersson (1992) found daycare experience gave children a better start in school. He examined the development of 128 children who attended neighbourhood daycare centres in Gothenburg where both low and middle income families routinely sent their children. Progress was monitored from the children's first year in daycare to the age of 13. No developmental disadvantage was found in the daycare group compared to children who had stayed at home. In fact, the highest performance in school tests and the best emotional adjustment was found in the children who had experienced the **most** daycare, even before the age of one year.

Why do Swedish children appear to benefit from attendance at childcare centres when British studies indicate that daycare attendance begins an inexorable slide towards poor school adjustment? Most likely the answer lies in different social policies, with Sweden offering highly subsidised daycare to families from all walks of life and Britain offering local authority daycare to 'problem families' only.

Research from the US, a country without 'progressive' daycare policy, provides further clues. Public daycare in the U.S. is usually of poor quality whereas private daycare, supported by families or voluntary agencies, tends towards better quality and is used by families with middle as well as low incomes. Howes (1988, 1990) studied 80 children in deliberately contrastive care. Half were enroled in excellent centres and half in poor ones. 'High quality' centres were characterised by the following: (a) stable childcare arrangements such that children interacted with just a few primary caregivers in any one day; (b) low staff turnover so that children were cared for by the same individuals over several years; (c) good staff training in child development, and (d) low adult:staff ratios, e.g. from 0-12 months the ratio was 1:3; from 1-3 years the ratio was 1:4, and from 4-6 years the ratio was 1:8-12.

All children who participated in the Howes' research were assessed for family background and individual differences so these could be controlled in the statistical analysis. With all scientific controls in place, the researchers found that children enroled in the higher quality centres did better later on in school on educational and social measures. The picture was different in the low quality centres, with children doing particularly poorly at school when they had been enroled in lower quality centres before their first birthdays. These children were distractible, low in task orientation and had considerable difficulty getting on with peers. Howes' research is rigorous because identical research methods were used on all the children and the same definition of 'quality' was applied throughout.

3.4   The social context of childcare

Research in both the U.S. and Sweden shows clearly that daycare for children over one year does not harm children if of high quality. In fact, the Swedish study suggests that daycare enhances children's development and gives them a better start in life. More recent, well controlled studies by Field (1991) point in the same direction. McGurk, Caplan, Hennessy and Moss (1993) argue persuasively that we cannot understand the effect of daycare on children's development without taking the cultural and social context *formally* into account in studies of outcome.

A theoretical framework for exploring the research findings of 'Mastery' orientation towards academic tasks

4   In 1985, Michael Rutter reviewed the literature on the effects of education on children's development and concluded that: 'The long term educational benefits stem not from what children are specifically taught but from effects on children's attitudes to learning, on their self esteem, and on their task orientation'. Nearly a decade later we can put in place some of the pieces unavailable when Rutter wrote his classic review. The most important impact of early education appears to be on children's aspirations, motivations and school commitment. These are moulded through experiences in the pre-school classroom which enable children to enter school with a positive outlook and begin a school career of commitment and social responsibility. Is there a theory of developmental psychology which can explain the patterns reviewed so far?

4.1   Children's explanations of academic success and failure:

For the past fifteen years a group of American psychologists has been exploring academic motivation and explanation via a series of ingenious experiments involving problem-solving. The bedrock of this work is an experimental procedure whereby children are given a series of tasks in which success is assured, followed by tasks designed to prompt failure. Dweck and Leggett (1988) found that children responded with two different patterns of behaviour when failure trials began. 'Mastery' oriented children maintained a positive orientation to the task and continued to employ problem-solving strategies. They were observed to monitor their strategies and showed positive affect throughout. From interviews it was clear that they viewed the difficult problems as challenges to be mastered through effort rather than indictments of their low ability.

In contrast, children characterised as 'helpless' in orientation began to chat about irrelevant topics, show a marked decline in problem-solving effort, and to show negative affect. These children appeared to view their difficulties as signs of their low ability; they rarely engaged in self-monitoring or self-instruction. Apparently one group of children saw the new, harder problems as an interesting challenge which could be overcome by effort and self instruction. The others viewed the new, more difficult problems as 'tests' of their innate ability and appeared convinced that they would fail. To summarise the results of the experiments:

★ Helpless children avoid challenge and give up easily, whereas mastery-oriented children persist in the face of obstacles and seek new, challenging experiences.

★ Helpless children report negative feelings and views of themselves when they meet obstacles while 'mastery' children have positive views of their competence and enjoy challenges.

★ The style of 'helpless' or 'mastery' oriented behaviour is not related to intelligence; rather it is a personality characteristic, a way of viewing oneself and one's capacity to be effective with things and people.

4.2   Learning v Mastery goals

Dweck and her colleagues have carried out scores of experiments along these lines with school-age children and adults. It seems clear that most individuals fall somewhere along a continuum of 'helplessness' to 'mastery' and that the behavioural patterns go hand in hand with a differing goal structure which children bring to the experiment. Further experiments revealed wholly different goal structures in children with the two different styles. Helpless children, it seemed, were pursuing performance goals which they sought to establish the adequacy of their ability and avoid showing evidence of inadequacy. They seemed to view achievement situations as tests of their competence and sought in such situations to be judged by others as competent. In contrast, mastery oriented children were pursuing learning goals in which the problem-solving tasks were just one more opportunity to acquire new skill.

To test the hypotheses (formed from interview data in the earlier experiments), the researchers deliberately manipulated children's goals of 'performance' or 'learning'. Elliott and Dweck (1988) set up classrooms, environments which shaped pupils towards performance or learning. Then they gave them opportunity to choose either challenging tasks or easy ones. The hypothesis was confirmed: children encouraged towards mastery goals chose challenging tasks when given the choice whereas children orientated towards performance goals chose the easy ones. The environmental manipulation proved effective, despite the children's 'real' skill and 'natural' inclinations.

Dweck summarised: 'What was most striking was the degree to which the manipulations created the entire constellation of performance, cognition, and affect characteristic of the naturally occurring achievement patterns'. For example, children who were encouraged towards performance orientation showed the same 'helpless' attributions, negative affect and strategy deterioration that characterised the helpless children in the original studies (Dweck and Leggett, 1988).

Dweck does not claim that it is always adaptive to believe oneself capable of intellectual tasks; indeed one needs to have an objective diagnosis of strengths and weaknesses in order to pursue one's goals effectively. However, adaptive individuals manage to co-ordinate performance and learning goals. An overconcern with proving oneself may lead the individual to ignore, avoid or abandon potentially valuable learning opportunities.

Thus, performance goals focus the student on judgements of ability and set in motion cognitive and affective processes that make the child vulnerable to maladaptive behaviour patterns. Learning goals create a focus on increasing ability and put into action cognitive and affective processes that promote adaptive seeking of challenge, persistence in the face of difficulty and sustained performance. These two differing goals underlie differing affects and behaviours in a variety of school-like tasks.

4.3   Malleability of intelligence

The last piece in the argument concerns studies by Bandura and Dweck (1985) and Leggett (1985) which all point to a link between mastery of orientation and the belief that intelligence is malleable. Their studies suggest that when children view intelligence as a malleable quality, learning goals come to the fore. These children believe that effort will lead to increased intelligence and tend to maintain persistence in the face of difficulty. Presumably this is because they view problem-solving or achievement outcomes as reflecting only effort or current strategy - not immutable talent. When children view intelligence as immutable, they show little effort ('a waste of time') and worry about the judgements of others (performance becomes crucial).

These patterns are well established by the age of nine or ten (Dweck and Leggett, 1988). But how do such adaptive and dysfunctional attributions begin and are they present at the very start of school? Many psychologists, especially those known as 'ego psychologists' (Erikson, 1963; White, 1959), have stressed that the young child strives for mastery. By middle childhood, however, many children have abandoned mastery behaviour in situations when negative outcomes are encountered (Diener & Dweck, 1978; 1980) and opt for performance ones instead.

Heyman, Dweck and Cain (1992) carried out a study to explore the affective reactions of children in kindergarten (five to six years of age). Children were asked to role play three scenarios, a neutral one and two in which a teacher criticises the child for errors in a play-task. Children were then interviewed and results showed that some of the five- and six-year-olds showed motivational patterns in response to teachers' criticism which were consistent with the 'helpless' orientation seen in older children. These children were described by the researchers as 'vulnerable to criticism'.

In subsequent interviews the vulnerable children viewed mistakes in the classroom as evidence that the perpetrator was 'bad' and that such 'badness' was immutable, not a temporary state. This important study suggests that vulnerability to teacher criticism can be seen at the age of five and that it is associated with the same views on the immutability of personal traits seen in older children with 'helpless' orientation. What is the origin of a belief in the immutability of individual traits? The worrying implication of this study is that some children are especially sensitive to teacher criticism from the earliest years at school. Perhaps linked to this is a naive nativism concerning global worth.

A cross cultural comparison concerning the themes of attribution of success and failure is beyond the scope of this review. However, there are several landmark studies (Stevenson and Lee, 1990; Stevenson, Lee, Chen and Lummis, 1990) on cross-national achievement in mathematics. In these, parental views about the mutability of intelligence have been sought. In a nutshell these investigators studied large samples of students in similar environments in the USA, China and Japan. They found that mathematics achievement was considerably lower in the USA than in the Asian countries. Of course they found that classroom experiences varied considerably across the countries. What is central to this review, however, is that parents in the two Asian countries appeared to believe that children's effort was crucial in school success, and *even more important than innate ability*. The Asian countries, perhaps influenced by the Confucian belief in human malleability, placed great weight on the possibility of children's advancement through effort. American parents, on the other hand, seemed quite satisfied with the mathematical progress of their children, expected less of them in terms of achievement, and passed on to their children the belief that 'natural talent' was more important in determining school grades than sheer hard work. 'An extreme interpretation of a nativist philosophy (in the USA) leads to two conclusions: first, the children of high ability need not work hard to achieve and, second, that children of low ability will not achieve regardless of how hard they work. The remarkable success of Japanese and Chinese students appears to be due in part to renunciation of these views ...'. The poor performance of the American children in this study was due to numerous factors, many of which are neither elusive nor subtle. Insufficient time and emphasis were devoted to academic activities; children's academic achievement was not a widely shared goal; children and their parents overestimated the children's accomplishments; parental standards for achievement were low; there was little involvement of parents in children's schoolwork; and an *emphasis on nativism* may have undermined the belief that all but seriously disabled children should be able to master the content of the school curriculum' (p103).

Curriculum for Mastery

5   Successful early education must do more than instil a few facts or simple cognitive skills. Its curriculum can be explicit about means to nurture positive beliefs about one's talents, and learning-orientation rather than performance-orientation. Pre-school learning must help children acquire resources for dealing with the stress of failure and the belief that achievement is not God-given but is, instead, acquired at least in part through effort.

We now come to the part of this paper which focuses closely on the theoretical underpinning of curriculum. For years, educationalists followed Piaget in his belief that what mattered most in early education was children's active exploration of objects; adults mattered little. The High/Scope programme (Hohmann, Banet & Weikart, 1979) which led to the impressive results described in Section 1.4 rests on Piaget but its originators also devised group conversational tasks which seem to have been inspired by Vygotsky (1962). Central is the *plan, do* and *review* cycle. In small groups with a teacher every child plans what she will do each day in a long session called 'work-time'. There is consideration of materials, play partners and sequence of events. After planning, the children go off to a defined area to carry out their plans. When finished, the small group reassembles and children take turns again, this time to review the outcome of their plans. The vital planning and reviewing takes place in conversation with the adult who supports and extends the child's work.

This special High/Scope dialogue is an embodiment of Vygotsky's notion of effective instruction within the zone of proximal development (Vygotsky, 1962; Sylva, 1992 b)). Each day, children are led towards the outer bounds of their own competence by a skilful tutor who encourages them to high aspiration, stimulates independence, and helps them look back on the fruits of their own plans.

How is this different from other pre-school curricula? The classic Piagetian curriculum centred on the child's lone exploration of the physical environment. Interaction mattered little, except for conflict, and adults played a minimum role. The High/Scope curriculum is specific in its means of developing a mastery or learning orientation. Its tutor-pupil interactions are explicit in the way they use language to guide the action in work-time, then to monitor and evaluate outcomes during the review session. The goal of the adult-child interaction is more than descriptive prose. It is a tutorial in using language to guide action and using reflection to be self-critical. Without fear children set high goals while seeking objective feedback on their plans. There is deliberate *modelling* in reflection on one's efforts. There is also encouragement to develop persistence in the face of failure and calm acceptance of errors or misjudgement. 'Today's feedback informs tomorrow's plan'.

Educational programmes similar to High/Scope are advocated by Dweck for older children to help them acquire mastery orientation. There are other pre-school programmes which move children in this direction, but High/Scope is explicit in the way the teacher uses the plan, do, review cycle to encourage mastery orientation. Perhaps the plan, do, review cycle is the cause of greater autonomy, commitment and aspirations seen by graduates of the High/Scope programmes demonstrated to be cost effective.

Does the quality of early learning matter?

6   This review has focused on the impact of early education on children's development. A few conclusions can be drawn:

a) The vast majority of research has shown that pre-school education leads to immediate, measurable gains in educational and social development.

b) The most rigorous studies show that *high quality* early education leads to lasting cognitive and social benefits in children which persist through adolescence and adulthood.

c) The impact of early education is found in all social groups but is strongest in children from disadvantaged backgrounds.

d) Investment in high quality early education 'pays off' in terms of later economic savings to society. Several studies show this.

e) The most important learning in pre-school concerns aspiration, task commitment, social skills and feelings of efficacy.

Acknowledgements

Mrs Jacqueline Wiltshire, Research Officer at the London Institute of Education, has contributed enormously to this review by her skilful library research and her determination to track down source materials no matter how obscure their publication.

References

Andersson, B.E. (1989). Effects of public daycare: a longitudinal study. *Child Development*, **60**, 857-866.

Andersson, B.E. (1992). Effects of daycare on cognitive and socioemotional competence of thirteen-year-old Swedish schoolchildren. *Child Development*, **63**, 20-36.

Bandura, A. & Dweck, C. (1985). The relationship of conceptions of intelligence and achievement goals to achievement-related cognition, affect and behaviour. Cited in: Dweck, C. & Leggett, E. (1988).

Barnett, W.S. & Escobar, C.M. (1990). Economic costs and benefits of early intervention, in: S.J. Meisels and J.P. Shonkoff (Eds.) *Handbook of Early Childhood Intervention* (pp. 560-583). Cambridge: Cambridge University Press.

Berrueta-Clement, J.R., Schweinhart, L.J., Barnett, W.S, Epstein, A.S. & Weikart, D.P. (1984). *Changed lives: the effects of the Perry pre-school programme on youths through age 19*. Ypsilanti, Michigan: The High/Scope Press.

Brophy, J., Statham, J. & Moss, P. (1992). *Playgroups in practice: self-help and public policy*. Department of Health. London: HMSO.

Bruner, J. (1980). *Under five in Britain*. London: McIntyre.

Campbell, D.T. & Erlebacher, A.E. (1970). How regression artifacts in quasi-experiment evaluations can mistakenly make compensatory education look harmful. In J. Hellmuth (Ed.) *Vol. 3, Disadvantaged child: compensatory education, a national debate*. New York: Brunner/Mazel.

Clark, M.M. (1988). *Children under five: educational research and evidence*. New York: Gordon and Breach Science Publishers.

Clarke-Stewart, K.A. (1988). Infant daycare: maligned or malignant? *American Psychologist*, **44**, 266-273.

Cochran, M.M. & Gunarsson, L. (1985). A follow-up study of group daycare and family-based childrearing patterns. *Journal of Marriage and the Family*, **47**, 297-309.

Diener, C.L. & Dweck, C.S. (1978). An analysis of learned helplessness: continuous changes in performance, strategy and achievement cognitions following failure. *Journal of Personality and Social Psychology*, **36** (5), 451-462.

Diener, C.L. & Dweck, C.S. (1980). An analysis of learned helplessness: II The processing of success. *Journal of Personality and Social Psychology*, **39**, 940-942.

Dweck, C.S. & Leggett, E. (1988). A social-cognitive approach to motivation and personality. *Psychological Review*, **95** (2), 256-273.

Elliott, E. & Dweck, C.S. (1988). Goals: An approach to motivation and achievement. *Journal of Personality and Social Psychology*, **54** (1), 5-12.

Erikson, E.H. (1963). *Childhood and society*. New York. W.W. Norton.

Field, T. (1991). Quality infant day-care and grade school behaviour and performance. *Child Development*, **62**, 863-870.

Goldberg, W. & Esterbrooks, M.A. (1988). Maternal employment when children are toddlers and kindergartners. In A.E. Gottfried and A.W. Gottfried (Eds.), *Maternal employment and children's development: longitudinal research*. New York: Plenum Press.

Heyman, G., Dweck, C. & Cain, K. (1992). Young children's vulnerability to self-blame and helplessness: relationship to beliefs about goodness. *Child Development*, **63,** 401-415.

Hohmann, M., Banet, B. & Weikart, D.P. (1979). *Young Children in action: a manual for pre-school educators*. Ypsilanti, Michigan. High/Scope Education Research Foundation.

Howes, C. (1990). Can the age of entry into childcare and the quality of childcare predict adjustment in kindergarten?. *Developmental Psychology*, **26**(2), 292-303.

Howes, C. (1988). Relations between early childcare and schooling. *Developmental Psychology*, **24**, 53-57.

Jowett, S. & Sylva, K. (1986). Does kind of pre-school matter? *Educational Research*, **28** (1), 21-31.

Kagan, J., Kearsley, R.B. & Zelazo, P.R. (1978). Infancy: its place in human development. Cambridge MA: Harvard University Press.

Lally, J.R., Mangione, P.L. & Honig, A.S. (1988). Long-term impact of an early intervention with low-income children and their families. In D.R. Powell (Ed.) *Vol. 4: Parent education as early childhood intervention: emerging directions in theory, research and practice*. Ablex, Hillsdale, N.J.

Lazar, I. & Darlington, R. (1982). The lasting effects of early education: a report from the Consortium for Longitudinal Studies. *Monographs of the Society for Research in Child Development*, **47** (2-3), serial no.195.

Lee, V., Brooks-Gunn, J. & Schnur, E. (1988). Does Head-Start work?. A 1-year follow up comparison of disadvantaged children attending Head-Start, no pre-school, and other pre-school programmes. *Developmental Psychology*, **24** (2), 210-222.

Leggett, E.L. (1985). Children's entity and incremental theories of intelligence: relationship to achievement behaviour. Cited in Dweck, C & Leggett, E.L. (1988).

Leggett, E.L. & Dweck, C.S. (1986). Goals and inference rules: sources of causal judgements. Cited in Dweck, C.S. and Leggett, E.L. (1988).

McGuire, J. & Richman, N. (1986). The prevalence of behaviour problems in three types of pre-school group. *Journal of Child Psychology and Psychiatry*, **27**, 455-472.

McGurk, H., Caplan, M., Hennessy, E. & Moss, P. (1993). Controversy, theory and social context in contemporary daycare research. *Journal of Child Psychology and Psychiatry*, **34** (1), 3-25.

McKey, H.R., Condelli, L., Ganson, H., Barrett, B., McConkey, C. & Plantz, M. (1985). *The Impact of Head Start on children, families and communities*. The Head Start Bureau, Administration for Children, Youth and Families., Office of Human Development Services. Washington, DC: CSR Incorporated.

Moore, T.W. (1975). Exclusive early mothering and its alternatives: the outcome to adolescence. *Scandinavian Journal of Psychology*, **16**, 255-272.

National Foundation for Educational Research Consortium (NFER) (1992). *An evaluation of the 1991 National Curriculum assessment, Report 4: the working of Standardised Assessment Tasks (SAT)*. NFER/BGC Consortium.

Osborn, A.F. & Milbank, J.E. (1987). The effects of early education: a report from the Child Health (1992). *Contemporary issues in the early years*. Paul Chapman Educational Series.

Porter, R. (1982). The effect of preschool experience and family environment on children's cognitive and social development. *Early Child Development and Care*, **9**, 155-174.

Rutter, M. (1985). Family and school influences on cognitive development. *Journal of Child Psychology*, **26** (5), 683-704.

Schweinhart, L., Weikart, D. & Larner, M. (1986). Consequences of three pre-school curriculum models through age 15. *Early Childhood Research Quarterly*. (1), 15-45.

Schweinhart, L.J. & Weikart, D.P. (1993). *A summary of significant benefits: The High Scope Perry pre-school study through age 27*. Ypsilanti, Michigan: High Scope UK.

Seitz, V., Rosenbaum, L.K. & Apfel, N.H. (1985) Effects of family support intervention: a ten-year follow-up. *Child Development*, **56**, 376-391.

Shorrocks, D., Daniels, S., Frobisher, L., Nelson, N., Waterson, A. & Bell, J. (1992). Enca 1 Project: The Evaluation of National Curriculum Assessment at Key Stage 1. School of Education, University of Leeds.

Smith, M.S. & Bissell, J.S. (1970). The impact of Head Start: The Westinghouse-Ohio Head Start evaluation. *Harvard Educational Review*, **40**, 51-104.

Smith, G. & James, T. (1977). The effect of pre-school education. In A.H. Halsey (Ed.), *Heredity and environment*, 288-311. London: Methuen.

Stevenson, H. & Lee, S. (1990) Contexts of achievement. *Monographs of the Society for Research in Child Development*, **55**(1-2), 1-119.

Stevenson, H., Lee, S., Chen, C. & Lummis, M. (1990). Mathematics achievement of children in China and the United States. *Child Development*, **61**, 1063-1066.

Sylva, K. (1992 a). Quality care for the under fives: is it worth it?. Edmund Rich Memorial Lecture. *RSA Journal*.

Sylva, K. (1992 b). Conversations in the nursery: how they contribute to aspirations and plans. *Language and Education*, **6**, 141-148.

Sylva, K., Siraj-Blatchford, I. & Johnson, S. (1992). The impact of the UK National Curriculum on pre-school practice: some 'top-down' processes at work. *International Journal of Early Education*, **24**, 40-53.

Turner, J.F. (1977). *Pre-school playgroup research and evaluation report*. Paper submitted to the DHSS in Northern Ireland.

Vygotsky, L. (1962). *Thoughts and Language*. MIT Press.

Valentine, J. (1979). Sargent Shriver. In E. Zigler and J. Valentine (Eds.), *Project Head Start: A legacy of war on poverty* (pp. 47-67). New York, Free Press.

Vandell, D.I. & Corasaniti, M.A. (1990). Variations in early childcare: do they predict subsequent social, emotional and cognitive differences?. *Early Childhood Research Quarterly*, **5**, 555-572.

Weiss, R.S. (1981). INREAL intervention for language handicapped and bilingual children. *Journal of the Division for Early Childhood*, **4**, 40-51.

Woodhead, M. (1989). Is early education effective? *British Journal of Educational Psychology*, **4**, 128-143.

White, R.W. (1959). Motivation re-considered: the concept of competence. *Psychological Review*, **66**, 297-333.

Zigler, E.F. (1987). Formal schooling for four year olds?: No. *American Psychologist*, **42**, 254-260.

APPENDIX D

A Summary of Significant Benefits: The High/Scope Perry Pre-School Study Through Age 27

by Lawrence J Schweinhart and David P Weikart

This Summary is reproduced with kind permission of the authors.

The High/Scope Research Institute, Ypsilanti, USA (1993)

High quality, active learning pre-school programs can help young children in poverty make a better transition from home to community and thus start them on paths to becoming economically self-sufficient, socially responsible adults. This was announced by the High/Scope Educational Research Foundation in a presentation at the Annual Meeting of Education Writers of America in Boston, Massachusetts, on April 18. The presentation made public for the first time the age 27 findings of the High/Scope Perry Project – a longitudinal pre-school effectiveness study now in its third decade.

This article, which reviews the study's cumulative findings and most recent conclusions, considers why some early childhood programs have long-term effects. It also examines the generalizability of this study's findings to other young children living in poverty and to other high quality, active learning pre-school programs. Finally, it discusses the policy implications of High/Scope's Perry study and similar studies.

Design of the Study

The High/Scope Perry Pre-School Project is a study assessing whether high-quality pre-school programs can provide both short and long-term benefits to children living in poverty and at high risk of failing in school. The study has followed into adulthood the lives of 123 such children from African American families who lived in the neighbourhood of the Perry Elementary School in Ypsilanti, Michigan, in the 1960s. At the study's outset, the youngsters were randomly divided into a *program group*, who received a high-quality, active learning pre-school program, and a *no-program group*, who received no pre-school program. Researchers then assessed the status of the two groups annually from ages 3 to 11, at ages 14–15, and at age 19, and most recently at age 27, on variables representing certain characteristics, abilities, attitudes, and types of performance. The median percentage of missing cases for these various assessments was only 4.9% and only 5% of cases were missing for the age-27 interviews. The study's design characteristics give it a high degree of internal validity, providing scientific confidence that the postprogram group-differences in performance and attitudes are actually effects of the pre-school program.

Figure 1.   *High/Scope Perry Preschool Study: Major findings at age 27. From Schweinhart and Weikart (1993).*

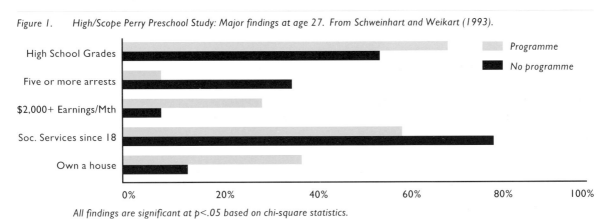

All findings are significant at p<.05 based on chi-square statistics.

As a group, the program females had significantly higher monthly earnings at age 27 than the no-program females (with 48% vs. 18% earning over $1,000) because more of the program females (80% vs. 55%) had found jobs. The program males, as a group, had significantly higher monthly earnings at age 27 than the no-program males (with 42% vs. 6% earning over $2,000) because the program males had better paying jobs. (Of employed males in the two groups 53% vs. 8%, respectively, were earning over $2,000, which is a significant difference.)

Certain other significant differences between the program group and the no-program group at age 27 were discovered to hold for males only or for females only. For example, compared with no-program females:-

* Significantly fewer program females, during their years in school, spent time in programs for educable mental impairment (8% vs. 37%).

* Significantly more program females completed 12th grade or higher (84% vs. 35%).

* Significantly more program females were married by age 27 (40% vs. 8%).

As compared with no-program males:-

* Significantly fewer program males received social services at some time between ages 18 and 27 (52% vs. 77%).

* Significantly fewer program males had 5 or more lifetime arrests (12% vs. 49%).

* Significantly more program males owned their own homes at age 27 (52% vs. 21%).

The findings listed here have economic values that prove to be benefits to society. Compared with the pre-school program's cost, these benefits make the program indeed a worthwhile investment for taxpayers and for society in general: *Over the lifetimes of the participants, the pre-school program returns to the public an estimated $7.16 for every dollar invested.*

Furthermore, the positive implications of the study's findings for *improved quality of life* for participants, their families, and the community at large are of tremendous importance.

Figure 2.   *High/Scope Perry Preschool study. Sources of public costs and benefits per participant. From Schweinhart and Weikart (1993)*

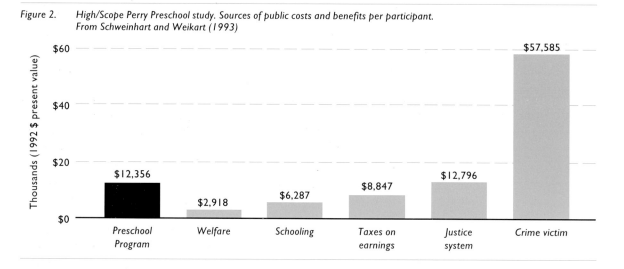

Educational-Performance Findings

Throughout the course of the longitudinal study, pre-school program effects were reflected in the educational performance of the pre-school program participants. Over the years, the program group produced significantly higher scores than the no-program group on tests of:-

* Intellectual performance (IQ) from the end of the first year of the pre-school program to the end of first grade at age 7

* School achievement at age 14

* General literacy at age 19

In addition, as compared with the no-program group, the program group:-

* Spent significantly fewer school years in programs for educable mental impairment (with 15% vs. 34% spending a year or more).

* Had a significantly higher percentage reporting at age 15 that their school work required preparation at home (68% vs. 40%).

Conclusions and Qualifications

At the end of almost three decades of research, five conclusions seem warranted.

1 Children's participation in a high-quality, active learning pre-school program at ages 3 and 4 created the framework for adult success, significantly alleviating the negative effects of childhood poverty on educational performance, social responsibility, adult economic status, and family formation.

2 The lives of both the program group and the no-program group have followed a predictable pattern of development since their early school years. Any subsequent intervention, such as school remediation, special education, or criminal justice measures, has not seemed to improve the life course of study participants. In particular, although grade retention and programs for educable mental impairment are intended to help youngsters, girls placed in these situations were nevertheless very likely to drop out before completing high school.

3 The effects of the pre-school program were different for females than for males during the school years. For females, the pre-school program appeared to create the interest and capacity to remain in school and graduate, in spite of difficulties presented by such problems as teen pregnancy. For males, the pre-school program appeared to affect not their likelihood of high school graduation , but their adjustment to society. The program seemed to create for them a chain of events that led to their assuming greater responsibility; this included a distinct lessening of criminal and other antisocial behaviour.

4 The essential process connecting early childhood experience to patterns of improved success in school and the community seemed to be the development of habits, traits, and dispositions that allowed the child to interact positively with other people and with tasks. This process was based neither on permanently improved intellectual performance nor on academic knowledge.

5 The lifetime economic benefits to the pre-school program participants, their families, and the community far outweigh the economic cost of their high-quality, active learning pre-school program. If this program had not been offered, the direct costs to society in lost labor-force participation, increased criminal behaviour, and additional welfare support would have far exceeded the program's costs.

Some *qualifications* must be added to the Perry's study's conclusions. First of all, we must keep in mind that the findings describe two groups, but not every individual in those groups. While some young people rose above their backgrounds to reach new levels of opportunity and performance, the improvements for most were incremental rather than radical. Although the significant differences between the program group and the no-program group are of extraordinary personal and social importance, not every program participant succeeded, and not every member of the no-program group failed. Even though it can be said that the pre-school program, by providing significant benefits, provided participants with a partial 'inoculation' against the negative effects of poverty, it cannot be said that the pre-school program in any sense offered a 'cure' for the problems of poverty.

A second qualification is this. As much as the High/Scope Perry Pre-School Project data support the extraordinary value of high-quality early education in breaking the cycle of poverty, pre-school programs are only one part of the solution. If the nation is to really confront poverty and its related problems of unemployment, welfare dependence, crime, and drug abuse, much broader social policy action is needed. Improved educational opportunities at all levels, access to medical care, affordable housing, effective job-training programs, elimination of institutional racism – all these must play a part, as well. The significance of the role of high-quality, active learning pre-school education should be neither overrated nor underrated.

A final qualification concerns the pre-school program itself. Special note should be taken that the pre-school program responsible for the effects talked about here had these four defining aspects of high quality:-

★ A developmentally appropriate, active learning curriculum

★ An organized system of in-service training and systematic, ongoing curriculum supervision

★ An efficient, workable method of parent inclusion and involvement

★ Good administration, including a valid and reliable, developmentally appropriate assessment procedure; a monitoring system; and a reasonable adult-child ratio.

High quality is essential if the promise of early childhood education is to be realized. While pre-service staff training, adequate staff salaries and benefits, appropriate space and materials, and health and nutrition services all contribute to the quality of a program, full realization of high quality requires an effective curriculum for the participating children and their families. There is probably nothing inherently beneficial about a program in which a child interacts with an extrafamilial adult and a group of peers each day; *a curriculum must be involved, to determine the program's organization and delivery*. It is long past time to insist that the delivery and organization of all early childhood programs meet standards of quality.

Why some pre-school programs have long-term effects

What makes a program experienced at ages 3 and 4 so powerful that it can change the pattern of children's lives, even when they reach adulthood? Why do the effects of early childhood experiences last a lifetime?

Early childhood, because of its timing in the child's physical, social, and mental development, is an opportune time to provide special experiences. Physically, pre-school-aged children have matured enough to have a fair amount of both fine and gross-motor co-ordination and to move about freely and easily; they are no longer toddlers. Socially, pre-schoolers have largely overcome any fears of strangers or of unfamiliar locations, and they usually welcome new settings and new interactions with peers and adults. Mentally, 3- and 4-year-olds have developed extensive ability to speak and understand and can use objects in a purposeful way. Piaget saw pre-school-aged children as in the preoperational stage – needing to learn from actual objects – and on the threshold of the concrete – operational stage – being able to learn from symbols and signs (Piaget and Inhelder, 1969). When children are fully concrete operational in thought processes at age 6 or 7, schools begin instruction in the sign/symbol-based skills of reading, writing and arithmetic.

‚Our best appraisal of the High/Scope Perry Pre-School Project results is this: *It was the development of specific personal and social traits that enabled a high-quality early childhood education program to significantly influence participants' adult performance*. Erikson (1950) pointed out that the typical psychological thrust of 3- to 5-year-olds is towards developing a sense of initiative, responsibility, and independence. Katz and Chard (1993), discussing the importance of children developing the dispositions of curiosity, friendliness, and co-operation, pointed out that good pre-school programs support the development of such traits. These personal dispositions cannot be directly taught, but they can develop under appropriate, active learning experiences. This suggests looking at specific circumstances and program strategies that support the development of such dispositions.

The pre-school program that was developed in the course of the Perry Project employed what today is known as the High-Scope Curriculum. It is a curriculum that relies heavily on active, child-initiated learning experiences during which children plan, or express their intentions; carry out their intentions in play experiences; and then reflect on their accomplishments.

These three elements of an active learning curriculum, – *children's expression of intent*, their *independently generated experiences*, and their *reflections* – are central to the definition of child-initiated learning. Outcomes of such learning include the development of traits important to lifelong learning – initiative, curiosity, trust, confidence, independence, responsibility, and divergent thinking. These traits, valued by society, are the foundations of effective, socially responsible adulthood.

When children participate in an active learning curriculum, they develop self-control and self-discipline. This control is *real power* – not over other people or materials, but over themselves. Understanding what is happening in the surrounding environment, realizing that those around them are genuinely interested in what they say and do, and knowing that their work and effort have a chance of leading to success give a sense of control that promotes personal satisfaction and motivates children to be productive. While no single factor assures success in life, the sense of personal control is certainly a major force. A high-quality, active learning pre-school program should support and strengthen this feeling.

Generalizability of the findings

We must carefully consider the generalizability of findings from the High/Scope Perry Pre-School Project (and of the findings from similar studies) if we are to make good use of the research. Some opponents of pre-school programs *undergeneralize* the Perry findings, whereas some proponents tend to *overgeneralize* them. Undergeneralizers say that the pre-school program involved had unique qualities that could not be duplicated elsewhere – that its cost was impractical, or that its operating conditions cannot be duplicated on a widespread basis or that teachers similarly qualified cannot be found today. Overgeneralizers claim that the Perry study established the long term benefits of Head Start or state pre-school programs or child day care programs – without considering the quality of any of these programs. Neither undergeneralizers nor overgeneralizers of the Perry study findings are contributing to the development of sound public policy.

Generalizing the findings of the High/Scope Perry Pre-School Project demands attention to two aspects of the project – its *participants* and its *program operation*. Replication of the characteristics of the participants *and* the characteristics of the program should lead to replication of the effects, within the study's intervals of statistical confidence. The question is, how broadly can we define the population and the program and still retain confidence that similar effects will result? Such definition requires careful judgement involving (1) selecting descriptive categories for the participants and for the program and (2) estimating what constitutes tolerable variation in these categories if replication of the original study is to be achieved.

For this purpose, we define the study participants as *people living in poverty*. We believe that generalization can be made across specific socioeconomic conditions within poverty, across specific ethnic groups, across specific times, and across specific locations within developed countries. Cautious generalization might even be made to certain locations within less developed countries.

For purpose of generalization and replication, we define the program as a *high-quality, active learning program for 3- and 4-year-olds*: a program designed to contribute to their development, with daily 2½-hour sessions for children Monday through Friday and weekly 1½-hour home visits to parents, and with 4 adults trained in early childhood education serving 20-25 children. It is reasonable to generalize program effects to other programs with these features, but again, the question lies in the degree of tolerance permitted in the variability of the program's features. Three sets of features will be considered here.

The first set of features concerns the sessions held daily for 20 to 25 children, and the parent outreach:-

★ Active learning: The active learning approach used in the children's classroom sessions and in the home visits should *encourage children to initiate their own developmentally appropriate activities*.

★ *Parent involvement*: The program should *include a substantial outreach effort to parents*, such as weekly home visits and parent group meetings, in which staff acknowledge and support parents as actual partners in the education of their children and model active learning principles for them.

A second set of features has to do with the program's timing and duration:-

★ *Age of Children*: The program should *serve children at ages 3 and 4*, the pre-school years prior to school entry.

★ *Program duration*: Children should attend the program for *two school years*; the evidence from this study for a program of only one school year is weak, based on only 13 program participants.

★ *Time per week*: The program should have *at least 12 ½ hours a week of classroom sessions for children* – 2 ½ hours a day, 5 days a week. An hour or so more or less should not matter. Even a full, 9-hour-a-day program, if it meets all the other standards of quality, would probably produce similar if not greater effects.

A third set of features has to do with the program's staffing, training and supervision:-

★ *Staff-child ratio*: The staff-child ratio should be *at least 1 adult for every 10 children and preferably for every 8 children*. While the Perry program had 4 adults for 20 to 25 children, the High/Scope Curriculum has since been used with very positive results in classes having 2 adults for as many as 20 young children (Epstein, 1993).

★ *Inservice training programs*: staff need *systematic training in early childhood development and education*.

★ *Staff supervision*: The Perry Project's teaching staff worked daily with supervisory staff in training and planning. Staff need *ongoing supervision by trained supervisors or consultants who know the curriculum* and can assist in its implementation by individual teachers and with individual children. Inservice training and curriculum supervision result in high-quality pre-school programs with significantly better outcomes for children (Epstein, 1993).

Pre-school programs that do not serve children living in poverty and that are not of high quality, within reasonable degrees of tolerance, cannot lay claim to replicating the program used in the High/Scope Perry Pre-School Project and thus are not likely to achieve its long-term effects.

Policy implications

The issue of insuring program quality (see Willer, 1990) should be central to the congressional and legislative debate on funding for Head Start and similar publicly sponsored pre-school programs. This need for quality was recognized in the last (1991) program authorization of Head Start, called the Head Start Quality Improvement Act. Because present funding levels do not allow these programs to serve all young children living in poverty, there is a danger that the debate will be framed solely in terms of expanding enrolment. Findings of the High/Scope Perry Pre-School Project and similar studies indicate that the congressional debate over increased funding for Head Start ought to be over how much to spend on quality improvement (especially training and assessment) versus program expansion. In light of the documented benefits of high-quality programs, it would be irresponsible to permit current programs to continue or expand without substantial efforts to improve and maintain their quality.

Fundamental to any effort to improve Head Start quality is widespread *formative assessment* of current Head Start program-implementation and outcomes for young children. This assessment must focus not only on the performance of teaching staff in implementing high-quality, active learning programs but also on the outcomes regarding young children's development. The assessment tools used should embody a vision of what such programs are about and what they can accomplish.

For the assessment of teaching staff, two such tools are the Early Childhood Environment Rating Scale (Harms & Clifford, 1980) and the High/Scope Program Implementation Profile (High/Scope Education Research Foundation,

1989; Epstein, 1993). One such tool for the assessment of young children's development is the High/Scope Child Observation Record (COR) for Ages 2½-6 (High/Scope Educational Research Foundation, 1992, Schweinhart, McNair, Barnes, & Larner, 1993). Assessment of young children's development needs to be consistent with principles of active learning and the cognitive, social, and physical goals of pre-school programs. Many evaluations, even by respected researchers, have been limited to narrow tests of intellectual and language performance, or worse, brief screening tests noted mainly for their brevity and inexpensiveness. Such tests, unfortunately, are only marginally related to the proper goals of high-quality pre-school programs.

Existing research has defined *the full potential of Head Start and similar programs*, establishing that programs – if they are done well – can improve children's success in school, increase their high school graduation rates, reduce their involvement in crime, and increase their adult earnings. But research findings fail to define the limits of program variation within which these extraordinary society goals can be realised, it is too easy for policy makers to ignore these limits.

Some examples, from state-funded pre-school programs, show how the process of ignoring the limits works. When, in Texas, it seemed politically feasible to establish a staff-child ratio of 1 to 22 in a program for at-risk 4-year-olds, state legislators did not challenge the adequacy of this ratio, fearing that any hesitation in supporting the program might have enabled the program's opponents to eliminate it altogether. When Michigan legislators planning to spend $1,000 per child on a new state pre-school program received expert testimony that the minimum cost for high-quality pre-school programs was $3,000 per child (a decade ago), they decided to increase Michigan's spending per pre-school child – to $2,000.

Based on existing knowledge, the standards of quality for Head Start and other publicly funded pre-school programs should be set high. But, because the nation has finite resources, research on the allowable limits of program variation should begin as soon as possible. One important area for 'limits research' would be staff-child ratios. This report recommends a staff-child ratio of at least 1 adult for every 10 children. Since existing research does not answer the question of whether one adult can deliver an effective program for more than this number of children, it would be unnecessarily risky at this time to operate large-scale programming with more than 10 children per adult – unless the programs were operated as part of experimental studies that provided new knowledge of the effectiveness of such programs.

Similarly, we need to prove the lower limits of teacher qualifications for delivery of effective pre-school programs. Surely effective programs require staff trained in early childhood development and education, but what level of training is required? Must all teaching staff have the same level of training? Many variations in staff training are possible. The unanswered question is, what would a well-designed research study be able to determine about minimal qualification?

Any of the other components of pre-school program quality presented in this article could, and should, be subjected to like scrutiny. There is widespread acceptance of the importance of an active learning curriculum for young children, but what should it look like? There is widespread acceptance of the importance of a strong outreach to parents, but the outreach described in this article focuses on the parent-child relationship, whereas some other forms of outreach have focused on the provision of various social services to parents. What is the proper balance?

The definition of pre-school program quality presented in this article is a research-based summary of what is most likely to help young children living in poverty to achieve the striking benefits reported here. But quality should have a dynamic definition, constantly under development, constantly being refined by the results of new research studies.

The most important public policy recommendation from this study and similar studies is a call for *full funding* for the national Head Start program and similar programs – enough to not only *serve all 3- and 4-year-olds living in poverty* but also *adequately serve each child*. Each eligible child should experience a *high-quality, active learning pre-school program*. The national Head Start program is where we should start. It is in place, with experienced teachers and administrators, and Congress has already authorized full funding for the program. But sufficient dollars for full funding have yet to be appropriated. Given the quality-of-life benefits as well as the economic return on investment found in this study and in similar pre-school effectiveness studies, the rationale for finding the dollars is compelling.

Footnotes A group difference identified as significant was found by the appropriate statistical test to be statistically significant with a two-tailed probability of less than .05.

Epstein (1993) found that high-quality programs using the High/Scope Curriculum developed in the High/Scope Perry Pre-School Project helped participating young children to achieve significantly higher scores than young children in other high-quality programs on the High/Scope Child Observation Record in initiative, social relations, creative representation, and music and movement; but these same children did not achieve higher scores on a screening test – Developmental Indicators for the Assessment of Learning, Revised (DIAL R, Mardell-C Zudnowski & Goldenberg, 1990).

Glossary

Early Childhood – encompasses broadly the first seven or eight years of life, which should be viewed as a continuum of development.

Early Learning – describes the development of children's capacity and motivation to acquire knowledge, skills and attitudes, to make sense of their world and to operate effectively within it. While cognitive development is a central element in this learning, it is essentially linked to children's all-round development - which occurs in both formal and informal settings.

Education – is not to be equated solely with schooling and goes beyond formal instruction in academic skills. In the early years, education is concerned with the promotion of a child's physical, social, emotional, spiritual and cognitive development and the establishment of positive attitudes to learning. It always includes an element of care (and an attitude of caring). Education also involves observation, assessment and planning to facilitate individual learning

Educators – are all adults (including parents) who contribute to, and are involved in, the education of the young.

Developmentally-appropriate practice – is both age-appropriate and individual-appropriate. Knowledge of typical child development patterns is used in conjunction with an understanding of individual children's unique patterns of growth and development (and the context in which this occurs) in order to design the most appropriate learning environment for each child, including those with severe learning difficulties.

The curriculum – includes *all* the activities and experiences (planned and unplanned, formal and informal, overt and hidden) from which a child learns. In its broadest form, the curriculum involves a consideration of the process of learning (how a child learns), the learning content (what a child learns), the learning progression (when a child learns) and the learning context (where and why a child learns). An educationally-explicit curriculum consists of the agreed concepts, knowledge, understanding, skills, experience, attitudes and values that it is intended that children should develop. It is this which guides professional practice, including assessment and planning.

Play – is a primary vehicle for learning. Through their play, children develop intellectually and also physically, emotionally and socially. Play gives children a sense of control in which they can consolidate their learning and try out developing skills and understanding. Children operate at the edge of their capacity in many play situations which may be enhanced and extended when a supportive adult is participating. 'Purposeful play' is central to the pre-school curriculum. 'The heart of learning in early childhood is a most serious playfulness.' (Bolton, 1989)

Skills – may be described as the capacity or competency to perform a task or activity. The education of young children involves developing a wide range of skills. Many may be applied in a variety of contexts, and in learning to apply them children gain satisfaction and grow in confidence. Examples include social skills, practical and physical skills, communication skills, study skills and investigative skills.

Concepts – are generalisations which help a child to classify, to organise knowledge and experiences, and to predict. Understanding and applying relevant concepts is an important part of the learning process. Examples of these include inside/outside, above/below, similar/different.

Attitudes – are expressions of values and personal qualities which determine behaviour in a variety of situations. These include respect, tolerance, independence, perseverance and curiosity. Such may be fostered in the curriculum and in the general life of the school.

A Curriculum for Early Learning

Professor Kathy Sylva, *Institute of Education, University of London*

A curriculum consists of concepts, knowledge, understanding, attitudes and skills that we wish children to develop. The National Curriculum specifies, for instance, that children around the age of seven should read simple signs and notices accurately and add or subtract up to ten objects. Although there is no curricular 'entitlement' for children under the age of five there is a welcome agreement amongst early years educators concerning the concepts, knowledge, understanding, attitudes and skills that we aim to foster in young children. This was summarised in the report of the Rumbold Committee (DES, 1990) who considered the early years curriculum to be the foundation on which education in the primary phase will build.

There is also an informal curriculum and this consists of important areas of learning about the self, the social environment and 'extra-curricular' aspects of the formal curriculum. Both the formal curriculum and the informal one which surrounds it are the responsibility of parents, teachers and the community. One difference between pre-school centres and the home is the explicit nature of the educational curriculum and agreed means for fostering it.

Broad aims of the early learning curriculum

HMI (1989) have made clear that the principles which underpin the education of older children are also relevant for those under five.

'Certain general principles that inform the planning and evaluation of the curriculum for children of compulsory school age hold true for the under fives. As for older pupils, the curriculum for young children needs to be broad, balanced, differentiated and relevant: to take into account the assessment of children's progress: to promote equal opportunities irrespective of gender, ethnic grouping or socio-economic background: and to respond effectively to children's special educational needs. The Education Reform Act calls for a balanced and broadly based curriculum which:

i   promotes the spiritual, moral, cultural, mental and physical development of pupils at the school and of society: and

ii   prepares such pupils for the opportunities, responsibilities and experiences of adult life.'

A curriculum framework

In *'Starting with Quality'* (1990) the Rumbold Committee describe the curriculum for children under five and suggest ways it can be taught most effectively.

'It is the educator's task to provide experiences which support, stimulate and structure a child's learning and to bring about a progression of understanding appropriate to the child's needs and abilities. Careful planning and development of the child's experiences, with sensitive and appropriate intervention by the educator, will help nurture an eagerness to learn as well as enabling the child to learn effectively.'

'We believe that, in fulfilling this task for the under fives, educators should guard against pressures which might lead them to over-concentration on formal teaching and upon the attainment of a specific set of targets. Research points to the importance of a broad range of experiences in developing young children's basic abilities.'

'The educator working with under fives must pay careful attention not just to the content of the child's learning, but also to the way in which that learning is offered to and experienced by the child, and the role of all those involved in the process. Children are affected by the *context* in which learning takes place, the *people* involved in it and the *values and beliefs* which are embedded in it.'

The Rumbold Report (1990) p.9

For the early years educator, therefore, the process of education - how children are encouraged to learn - is as important as, and inseparable from the content - what they learn.

The framework, adopted by the Rumbold Committee followed the one put forward by HMI in their 1985 discussion document *The Curriculum from 5 to 16*. This embodies nine areas of experience and learning: aesthetic and creative, human and social, linguistics, mathematical, physical, scientific, moral, technological and spiritual.

Areas of learning experience (from the Rumbold Report, 1990, pp.38-45)

Aesthetic and creative

Art, craft, design, music, dance and drama promote the development of young children's imagination and their ability to use media and materials creatively and to begin to appreciate beauty and fitness for purpose.

From an early age children enjoy and respond to sensory experience. They explore and experiment with materials, making patterns, pictures and models; they make sounds and music; they engage in role-play and drama; and make up mimes and movement sequences. They also listen to music, sometimes responding rhythmically, sometimes quietly entranced; they listen to poems, songs and rhymes learning to appreciate the sounds and rhythms of the words; they look at pictures and other works of art, at buildings and bridges and begin to develop their aesthetic awareness and understanding.

Human and social

For young children human and social learning and experience is concerned with people, both now and in the past, and how and where they live. It is the earliest stage in the development of skills and ideas necessary to the understanding of history and geography.

Young children are naturally interested in people, in their families and homes and the community in which they live. From an early age they are aware of the work that members of their families do and often reflect this in their role-play. Adults can help children to gain greater understanding of the lives of others by providing appropriate resources for such play. Learning through play, and through other experiences such as visits to various workplaces, about the lives of shopkeepers, nurses, doctors, police officers and others provides an important foundation for the later understanding of the interdependence of communities.

Many young children are curious about the past. They are interested in old objects; in what things were like when their parents, teachers and helpers were children; and in what they were like as babies. Adults can help satisfy this curiosity, and in so doing help children to develop a sense of time and change, by providing collections of artefacts from bygone days; inviting older people to tell the children about their early lives; and by talking about events in their own lives, and those of the children and their families.

Language and literacy

This fundamentally important area of the curriculum for the under fives may be usefully sub-divided into four modes; speaking, listening, reading and writing. Most children will be adept speakers and listeners by the time they enter pre-school provision. Many will be familiar with favourite stories read to them at home. They will have learned nursery rhymes and TV jingles. Some may be able to recognise their own name in print and be capable of writing it or making marks on paper which closely resemble words. A few children may be capable of reading and writing simple sentences.

Given the wide range of differences in their performance on entry to pre-school provision those who teach them will need to assess the children's existing competence for the purpose of planning a language programme with continuity and progression in mind.

Adults working with under fives are well placed to observe and record their responses on a day to day basis and to judge their language needs accordingly. For children of this age the balance of language activities across the four modes is likely to be weighted in favour of speaking and listening. This is achieved on a one-to-one basis between a child and an adult, through language activities in small groups and sometimes between an adult and all, or nearly all, the children in a whole class or playgroup. For example, a good story read by an adult from a well illustrated book may engage the attention of a whole group or class. In these circumstances, although the children may be at very different levels of language competence, well chosen literature enables the adult to link the spoken and the written word in a context of high interest and to fire the children's imagination. In this way experience is shared and listening and speaking are intensified. Similar outcomes stem from common experiences provided, for example, in singing, moving to music or from visits to places of interest.

Mathematics

Young children's experiences provide a ready basis for learning mathematical ideas. Regular events such as climbing stairs, preparing meals, singing nursery rhymes, shopping and travelling by bus or car, provide early opportunities for children to learn to count and use mathematical symbols. For example, some children aged two can answer 'How many fish fingers do you want?' with an appropriate response - 'Lots', 'None', 'Two'. Using words and other symbols to convey ideas of quantity is important to children's early mathematical experiences. The gradual transition from the use of words such as 'lots', 'big', 'heavy' to more precise mathematical vocabulary in correct contexts - 'we need 100 grams of flour' - is an important competence that young children begin to acquire in pre-school provision.

For the purpose of extending their mathematical experiences learning can be planned within five broad areas: shape; space and position; patterns and relationships; comparison (measures); and numeracy. The relationship between practical activity and the development of an appropriate language to support the understanding of mathematical ideas is central to this area of the curriculum.

All children need to learn a variety of mathematical concepts and processes if they are to understand and appreciate relationships and patterns in both shape and number, and to describe them clearly and precisely. An important element of young children's mathematical development is the exploration of everyday materials and equipment. Through using materials such as bricks, boxes and construction kits, children develop basic ideas of shape, space and position. When adults share and discuss these experiences using appropriate mathematical terminology, young children readily learn to refer confidently, for example, to edges, corners, surfaces and elevation.

Physical
The area of physical learning and experience for young children is concerned with developing manipulative and motor skills, physical control, co-ordination and mobility. It involves knowledge of how the body works and establishes positive attitudes towards a healthy and active way of life.

Young children usually show great interest in increasing their own physical skills and often exploit opportunities adventurously. Effective pre-school provision builds on these trends through indoor and outdoor activities that are safe while encouraging the children to respond confidently to physical challenges.

Science
Well before the age of five, most children show interest in a wide range of biological and physical phenomena. For example, they are easily engaged in play with sand and water. They mix colours and investigate the properties of materials. They quickly learn that some materials are hard and others are soft, some are flexible and others are rigid. They notice that heat changes things, that ice melts and that light comes from different sources such as wax candles and electric bulbs. They take delight in caring for living things and watching how animals and plants behave. They watch the action of automatic washing machines and microwave cooking. Many will see their parents and older brothers and sisters using pocket calculators and home computers, and possibly be encouraged to do so themselves.

Spiritual and moral
Most children have the support of caring families through which they are helped to develop self confidence and an understanding of right and wrong. Some, however, are less fortunate and will have undergone abnormally stressful, emotional and social experiences in their family lives that hinder their development.

Children's experiences in their immediate and extended families provide a basis from which the adults working with under fives can help them to explore ideas, for example, of fairness, forgiveness, sharing, dependence and independence. Everyday educational activities, including the use of stories, rhymes and songs, enable children to work co-operatively and to take responsibility for their own actions.

Effective provision for the spiritual and moral areas of learning and experience is concerned with developing understanding about the significance and quality of human life and the formation of social and personal values. It secures an ethos in which under fives can reconcile social and emotional conflicts and build good interpersonal relationships.

By the age of three or four, most children will have taken part in celebrations and ceremonies such as birthdays and marriages. Some will have joined in religious celebrations such as Christmas, Divali, Eid-ul-Fitr or Hanukkah and be aware of the rituals or special goods associated with them. Some may come from homes where prayers and readings from religious literature are everyday events. Festivals often provide valuable opportunities for under fives to share celebrations with parents and other members of the community. Through these events children hear religious language, take part in role play and drama, and begin to gain some understanding of the importance of religion in people's lives.

Technology
As with science, young children will meet technology in many forms before they enter pre-school provision. In their homes they are likely to have used the remote control to switch on the television or video; they may have seen microwave ovens, digital clocks and push-button telephones; and they may have played with calculators or used computers for games or even simple educational programmes. Effective pre-school provision takes account of the children's interest in such equipment and develops it through the provision made for imaginative and investigative play including telephones, programmable toys and remote control cars. In some instances the children's experience of music is extended through the use of simple electronic keyboards. With careful guidance some chil-

dren are able to use computers in their pre-school group. Some see their cakes baked in a microwave oven and help to set the controls. All of these experiences develop their physical dexterity and further their interest in, and understanding of, technology.

Analysing the curriculum in these terms can help to ensure appropriate breadth and balance and to achieve continuity with the National Curriculum. It does not follow that the way in which the work is organised and experienced will adhere to this analytical framework. Thus, aspects of different areas of learning may be grouped together and integrated in a 'cross-curricular' approach. What is of prime importance is that the curriculum should be coherent in terms of the child's existing knowledge, understanding and skills and that it should be experienced in an environment which fosters the development of social relationships and positive attitudes to learning and behaviour.

Success, self esteem and resilience

Although not included by Rumbold or HMI as a separate 'area of experience', the early years curriculum also aims at the development of self esteem and resilience. Dowling (1992) describes how pre-school education shapes attitude toward the self.

'Nursery teachers accept that young children make mistakes and learn valuable lessons in this way. Children must also learn that in many ways there are no right or wrong answers. However, to foster children who are confident to 'have a go' and express their views, and eager to explore new learning, a nursery curriculum must allow experience of success and for these successful experiences to outweigh all others. The learning offered must therefore be manageable and broken into manageable parts. The great skill of teaching at any level is to facilitate learning – to identify what has been previously learnt and the next required step in learning: to find the right match of curriculum content and the appropriate learning route.'

'The beliefs children have about themselves will not only affect what they can do but also how they react to others. Because this belief is so closely linked with the individual's perceptions of how others view him or her, parents and teachers have a particularly powerful role to play with young children. It is particularly important that nursery teachers are aware of the need to support children who are members of groups that might encounter discrimination.'

'Carefully monitored group activity enables children to grow from an egocentric state to become group members. In their play children learn to lead, to follow and to co-operate, to wait and take turns. Opportunities for this type of growth need to be an integral part of a nursery programme.'

'Nurseries need to provide a climate in which a young child can develop emotional resilience and become socially and physically confident before the child can develop his or her thinking skills. Helping young children to take responsibility for their actions involves them in making choices and decisions. They need to be helped to take an increasingly active part in their own learning, and the teacher's planning and provision can assist this process.'

Effective curriculum planning and implementation

Effective curriculum planning and implementation requires common and clearly-understood aims, objectives and values. These are the basis on which is built the framework of attitudes, expectations, relationships and physical environment which children – and their parents – will experience.

Planning the curriculum

Lally (1989) explains why planning is crucial at nursery stage: 'Within any group of three to five year olds there will be huge variations in development, and a six month age difference between children at this stage is developmentally much more significant than a similar age difference between older children. For this reason it is vital that a curriculum for the under fives is planned'.

The Rumbold Report (p.10) states that

'Successful curriculum planning involves clear perceptions about the various objectives of the curriculum and how different activities can contribute to their achievement. But curriculum planning is not a once-and-for-all operation: it is a continuous cycle involving planning, observing, recording, assessing and returning to planning in the light of the intermediate stages'.

'An important element is an understanding of the interests and abilities which each child brings from home and from other early experiences. Parents have an important role in imparting detailed information as a basis for the educator's initial planning of provision which is appropriate to the child's interests, experience and abilities. Thereafter, the planning process needs to be sufficiently flexible and responsive to build on new learning possibilities as these emerge.'

Implementing the curriculum

Implementation is essentially the process of using resources of various kinds to achieve planned educational objectives. It requires:

(a) Agreed approaches to learning

Although young children learn in a number of ways, including exploring, observing and listening, Neil Bolton sums it up neatly: 'The heart of learning in early childhood is a most serious playfulness' (1989).

Lally (1991) argues that: 'Play as a learning process has the potential to fulfil all the nursery teacher's aims for children's development because it offers a way of motivating and interesting children in a broad curriculum. Play only reaches the full potential, however, if it is carefully planned and resourced, and if the adult has a clear role within it'.

The Rumbold Report (p.12) delves into more detail:

> '*Play* underlies a great deal of young children's learning. For its potential value to be realised a number of conditions need to be fulfilled:
>
> i   sensitive, knowledgeable and informed adult involvement and intervention;
>
> ii   careful planning and organisation of play settings in order to provide for, and extend, learning;
>
> iii   enough time for children to develop their play;
>
> iv   careful observation of children's activities to facilitate assessment and planning for progression and continuity.'

HMI (1989) add:

> 'Play that is well planned and pleasurable helps children to think, to increase their understanding and to improve their language competence. It allows children to be creative, to explore and investigate materials, to experiment and to draw and test their conclusions... Such experience is important in catching and sustaining children's interests and motivating their learning as individuals and in co-operation with others.'

(b) Curriculum integration

> 'Our (Rumbold Committee, p.13) preferred approach to analysis and planning of the curriculum through a framework of 'areas of experience' is intended to help educators see the potential for learning in the whole range of children's activities, both planned and spontaneous, and to encourage breadth and balance in the curriculum. For the child, however, the curriculum is more likely to be experienced through a variety of broadly-based experiences. Many activities, play settings and other routines provided by the educator will relate to several aspects of learning.'

(c) Review of the curriculum

> 'Curriculum planning is a continuous process. The curriculum is dynamic, and needs to be adapted in the light of practical experience, changing needs and increased knowledge. Educators must therefore build into the planning cycle a broad review of the effectiveness and value of the provision they make; extending beyond the immediate setting to include parent and community links, admissions policies, continuity, staff development and other factors which impinge on provision.'

(d) Continuity and progression

> 'Continuity and progression are interlinked concepts relating to the nature and quality of children's learning experiences over time. Progression is essentially the sequence built into children's learning through curriculum policies and schemes of work so that later learning builds on knowledge, skills understanding and attitudes learned previously. Continuity refers to the nature of the curriculum experienced by children as they transfer from one setting to another, be it from home to playgroup, from playgroup to school, from class to class within a school or from one school to another. Continuity occurs when there is an acceptable match of curriculum and approach, allowing appropriate progression in children's learning. Effective assessment and record keeping systems are the keys to these ends.'

Partnership with parents

Lally (1989) points out that effective partnership with parents requires high levels of training. 'Early years educators need well-developed interpersonal skills to enable them to work in partnership with parents, children and colleagues. These skills must include the ability to look critically at themselves and at their practice since it is vital that they are able to recognise the effect their own prejudices and stereotyped ideas can have on their expectations of families and children. The messages about themselves and their families which children receive both directly and indirectly within an educational setting form a powerful part of the curriculum. These complex skills and attitudes can only be developed by carefully planned, relevant, initial *and* in-service training'.

The Education, Science and Arts Select Committee (1989) concluded that: 'Parental involvement will take many different forms, ranging from discussion at open evenings through working with a child at home, or direct participation in the teaching and learning process, to assessing and diagnosing children's needs. Parents may also be involved in the management of services for the under fives, for example through membership of governing bodies or local under fives committees. What is always necessary, however, is the establishment of a partnership between parents and other educators. For this to be effective, there must be mutual understanding and respect, a continuing dialogue and sharing of expertise and information.'

References

Bolton, N. (1989) Developmental psychology and the early years curriculum. In C.M. Desforges (Ed.), 'Early childhood education', *The British Journal of Educational Psychology. Monograph 4* (pp41-46). Edinburgh: Scottish Academic Press.

Department of Education and Science (1990) The Rumbold Report. *Starting with Quality*, (pp36-45). London: HMSO.

Department of Education and Science. (1989). *Aspects of Primary Education. The education of children under five*, (p9). London: HMSO.

Dowling, M. (1992). *Education 3-5*, (chs. 3 & 4). London: Paul Chapman Publishing Ltd.

Lally, M. (1991). *The nursery teacher in action*, (ch.3, pp.70-82). London: Paul Chapman Publishing Ltd.

National Children's Bureau. (1989). *Curriculum for three to five year olds*. Highlight no. 89. London: National Children's Bureau.

APPENDIX F

Statistics on Early Childhood Services

Placing Britain in an international context

Peter Moss, *Thomas Coram Research Unit, University of London*

This short note consists of three parts: first, a short review of some of the major problems in constructing and interpreting cross-national league tables; second, a summary of some of the salient features of 'early childhood care and education services' in Britain, in particular the distinctive features compared to other countries; and third, an annotated table of participation in 'early childhood care and education services' for children between 3 and 5.

January 1994

I. Some problems in cross-national league tables

In recent years, there have been a number of attempts to construct 'league tables', providing cross-national comparisons of levels of provision in services for young children (for example, by the EC Childcare Network (1990), the Government Statistical Service (1993), OECD (1993)). While they meet a need amongst many, especially in the media, for instant comparisons, they are in many ways unsatisfactory, providing a limited or even misleading picture of the extent and nature of differences between countries.

There are four main problems with constructing and interpreting league tables.

I. Age range covered

The age of the start of compulsory schooling varies between countries from 5 to 7 (although 6 is the most common age). This raises the issue of what is the appropriate upper age limit for the league table. If you take the age at which compulsory schooling begins, then countries where children start early may object that this excludes the fact that all of their 5-year-olds are receiving a service (i.e.compulsory primary schooling). If you decide on a common upper limit (say 6), then it distorts the extent of 'pre-primary school' provision for countries which start compulsory schooling before 6.

A more profound issue, however, is posed by the lower age level chosen for presenting statistics. The Table in the EC Childcare Network report is for 'publicly funded childcare services' and covers provision for children from birth upwards (including schooling for children below compulsory school age). The Table in the report from the Government Statistical Service is of 'participation in education of 3- to 5-year-olds', the lower age limit reflecting the age at which children in the UK may start nursery education. But in some countries (e.g.Belgium, France), children start attending nursery school at 2, and the OECD Table, of 'early childhood education', takes 2 as its lower age limit.

The very fact of setting a lower age limit in tables of 'education' services for young children is based on a particular assumption, ie. that 'early childhood education' and services providing it only begin at a certain age - before which children can only receive 'care'. This assumption is not universally accepted, and has been specifically rejected in a number of places. In the Nordic countries, Spain, New Zealand, and in parts of some countries (e.g.Italy, UK) services for all children under compulsory school age have been integrated so that they are the responsibility of one department and on the basis that 'care and education are inseparable' with no lower limit on when learning can occur.

For example, the major education law adopted in Spain in 1990 (*Ley de Ordenacion General del Sistema Educativo* - LOGSE) introduces a radical new approach to services for children from 0-6:

"The LOGSE regulates children's education from infancy to the age of eighteen. Education is organised into three stages: Early Childhood Education (age 0-6), Primary Education (age 6-12) and Secondary Education (age 12-18)...As a result of long-term pressure rooted in the past and the Socialist Party's participation in Government from 1982 onwards, children from 0-6 have finally been included in the Spanish education system. The

Law makes the national Ministry of Education and Departments of Education in Autonomous Communities with jurisdiction over education responsible for *all* services for children from 0-6, which include nursery education in schools, nurseries for children under 4 and centres taking children from 0-6 (these nurseries and centres are renamed 'infant schools' (*escuela infantil*))" (Balaguer, 1993; 45,46).

2. 'Education' and 'daycare'

Even if statistics are limited to 'over 3s', a further problem arises about what services to include, especially if a cross-national review purports to concentrate on 'education'. In countries with a universal system of nursery schooling from age 3 there is little problem: all (or nearly all) children are to be found in one service that clearly fits into an 'educational' model. But not all countries are so obliging to the constructor of tables.

In a number of countries (for example, the Nordic countries and Germany) children attend services which are not called schools (instead they are called 'kindergartens', 'daghem', 'integrerede institutioner' etc), are generally outside the education system (being the responsibility usually of 'social welfare' departments) and which do not employ 'teachers'; these services however have clear pedagogical objectives and employ relatively well trained staff. Matters are further complicated because in some of these countries, there are also classes in primary schools for children to attend in the year before compulsory schooling; for example, nearly all 6-year-olds attend these 'kindergarten classes' in Denmark.

This different tradition in providing for young children creates problems for some cross-national comparisons of 'education'. The OECD review of 'early childhood education' only gives statistics for 6-year-olds in school for Denmark and Sweden; for 3- to 5-year-olds, it says that '*problems of definition render the calculation of participation rates infeasible (sic)*'. The table provided by the Government Statistical Service (which does not include 6-year-olds) offers no data on Denmark. Statistics for the other Nordic countries are divided between 'education' and 'daycare' in a way that is impossible to understand and which applies a false dichotomy on services which are in fact integrated in concept and structure.

Most countries have a divided system for children from 0-6. Mostly, the division is structured around age, with younger children (under 2 or 3) the responsibility of 'social welfare' authorities and older children the responsibility of education. In a few countries however, there is a welfare/education division within the same age group. Prominent examples are Greece, Portugal, Ireland and UK. Here the problem is to know whether and how to represent this split statistically. OECD, for example, appears to exclude services that are the responsibility of health/welfare departments in the UK and Ireland (e.g.playgroups, nurseries); but it combines education and welfare services for Portugal - and gives no data for Greece. The Government Statistical Service divides services into 'education' and 'daycare'; it provides no data for Greece or Portugal, but for Ireland and UK appears to put services that are the responsibility of health/welfare departments under 'daycare'.

Dividing services between 'education' and 'daycare' may be misleading (as in the case of the Nordic countries). Alternatively, it may be of little practical help since it gives no indications of the actual differences between services included under the two broad headings (except that they may be the responsibility of different government departments). Services included under 'daycare' may vary considerably between and within countries.

3. What services offer

League tables which boil down very different services in each country into a single number, or set of numbers, provide only the most limited basis for cross-national comparison. Even as measures of quantity of provision they are seriously deficient. For example, they say nothing about the length of time that services are available or children attend. In practice, there are big differences. Services in Denmark and Sweden (for children from 0-6) are open 9-10 hours a day, throughout the year, although children on average attend only 7 hours a day; nursery schools in France and Italy are mostly open more than 7 hours a day but only in term-time; most kindergartens in Germany are open 4-6 hours a day during term-time, but some are open for at least 8 hours a day; nursery classes and schools in England are open 6 hours a day, also in term-time only, but 89% of children attend on a part-time basis (i.e. less than 3 hours a day).

The statistics also say nothing about the types of services attended. There is the distinction between schools and other types of centre-based service (kindergartens, nurseries, playgroups etc.). Within schools there are distinctions: nursery education may be provided in separate 'nursery schools' or in classes attached to primary schools. In a very few countries (mainly UK and Ireland) much 'early childhood education' for children over 3 is provided by children being admitted early to primary school; in fact the Government Statistical Service statistics for Ireland, which show 51% of Irish 3- to 5-year-olds in 'education', consist entirely of this type of provision in which many children are provided for in classes with a child:teacher ratio of 35:1.

There are a wide range of other, more qualitative differences. Most notably, there are wide variations in staffing - numbers and ratios, training and qualifications, pay and conditions. These are most apparent among 'non-school' services especially for children under 3; in general, staff training, pay and conditions in these services are much inferior to that in 'nursery schooling'. For over 3-year-olds, the distinctions are most obvious between 'nursery schooling' and 'playgroups'; the latter usually have better adult:child ratios, but levels of training, pay and conditions are very much inferior. Major variations occur not only between services in the same country, but between different countries.

Without taking all these factors into account, it is possible (and has occurred in published DfE cross-national statistics) to create a table where a child attending a playgroup in the UK is presented as equivalent to a child attending a kindergarten in Denmark or a nursery school in France or Italy, even though there are in fact enormous differences in the hours of opening and attendance and the training and conditions of the staff.

4. Public funding

Public funding of a substantial part of the cost of services is critical if there is concern with issues of access and quality. There are of course major questions concerning how the costs of children should be allocated, as between parents and the wider society. But ignoring these for the moment, 'early childhood care and education services' without substantial public subsidy will either be inaccessible to many families or else, to bring their costs down, will have to compromise on conditions that have been shown to be associated with quality (e.g.staff numbers, training, pay, conditions etc.) and/or offer only very limited hours of provision.

In many countries, all (or a large proportion) of the provision for children over 3 is wholly or largely subsidised from public funds, either through the education budget where there is a system of nursery schooling or through the welfare budget in Germany and Nordic countries. Several countries have made commitments to extend publicly funded services, for example to guarantee places for all children over 3 in the case of Germany and Spain and for all children from the time Parental Leave finishes to compulsory school age in Denmark and Norway. Portugal has relatively under-developed services, but is expanding them to try and meet a goal of 80% of 5-year-olds and 40% of 3- and 4-year-olds in publicly-funded services by 1994.

Apart from Portugal, publicly funded services for children over 3 are less well developed in four countries. Netherlands and Luxembourg have no schooling for 3-year-olds, but universal provision for 4- and 5-year-olds; Ireland has virtually no schooling for 3-year-olds, but admits 4- and 5-year-olds early to primary school; the UK has limited schooling for 3- and 4-year-olds, much of which is provided in reception classes, with compulsory schooling for 5-year-olds. To fill this gap in publicly funded services for children over 3, which is particularly large for 3-year-olds, Ireland, Netherlands and UK rely heavily on playgroups, but only in the Netherlands do most playgroups receive some public funding and this only covers about half of their costs.

In general, public subsidy is much lower for services for children under 3. With the exception of the Nordic countries, most children under 3 receiving services depend either on relatives or on services for which most or all of the cost is borne by parents. *One of the consequences of this is that it is virtually impossible to make cross-national comparisons of services for children under 3.*

Data on attendance at non-subsidised services is usually non-existent or provided irregularly through 'household-based' surveys. Where data on these services is regularly published it is usually in the form of 'places available', rather than 'children attending'. For example, in the UK, DoH statistics on 'Day Care' provide information on *places and children* attending for local authority day nurseries but only on *places* for other, private services; by contrast, DfE statistics on schools provide information on pupils attending but not on places provided. Finally, it should be noted that where statistics are available on services for children under 3, account should be taken of the availability and use of Parental Leave since this may affect the age at which parents want and seek services; for example, in Sweden, the average age at which children are admitted to services has increased steadily as paid Parental Leave has been extended, and now that Leave lasts for 15 months it is unusual to find children in publicly funded services before the age of 15-18 months.

---

2.   Salient features of early childhood care and education services in Britain

*   *Responsibility for services is divided between Education and Social Services.* Such a division is not unusual internationally. In some countries, the division is based on age, with 'welfare' responsible for under 3s, 'education' for 'over 3s'. The UK follows the other approach, with 'welfare' responsible for under 3s, and services for over 3s divided between 'welfare' and 'education'; a similar situation is found in Greece and Portugal.

*   In 1991 in *Britain*, there were *places for approximately 1.43 million children under 5* in 'early childhood care and education services' - 867,000 in services that are the responsibility of Social Services/DoH ('daycare' services) and 563,000 in schools (maintained and private)[1].

---

1   Statistics on schools are for pupils attending part-time and full-time. Places have been calculated by assuming that there is one place for every two part-time pupils attending.

★ *Many of these places are used on a part-time or shift basis.* This increases the number of children receiving a service, but means that many children attend for relatively short periods of time. For example:

> 35% of school places are used on a part-time basis (ie. for a morning or afternoon session), and part-time pupils account for 51% of all pupils attending; 563,000 places are used by 758,000 pupils. Part-time pupils account for 88% of all pupils attending nursery education in maintained schools.

> Each place in English playgroups in 1992 was used, on average, by 1.8 children[2]. Since the 'average' playgroup was open for 4.6 half-day sessions per week, the 'average' child attends for only 2-3 sessions per week (or for 5-9 hours a week). This implies that the 409,000 registered playgroup places in England in 1992 were used by over 730,000 children.

★ The 1986 General Household Survey (GHS) study of use of services for children under 5 found that 76% of children attended services for 5 half days or less per week, and *nearly half went for 3 half days or less* (for further details see OPCS, 1989). The 1991 GHS, which included 'unpaid family and friends', shows a similar picture, with 59% of children receiving 10 hours or less of 'care' per week and a further 22% receiving 11-20 hours; for 'schools' the figures were 38% and 36% respectively, and for 'private or voluntary schemes' (which would have included playgroups), 85% and 8% respectively (Bridgwood and Savage, 1993; Table 7.11).

★ Most children attending 'schools' (93%) go to publicly-funded maintained provision. Although it is impossible to be as precise about 'daycare' services, a conservative estimate would suggest that at least 85% of children and places, and probably over 90%, depend wholly or mainly on parental fees. This means that *over half of children under 5 attending services go to unsubsidised provision* (playgroups, childminders, private nurseries and schools) and the proportion is growing.

★ There are no recent published data on the *type of services attended by children* in the age groups 0-2, 3-4 or indeed over the full 0-4 age range. The categories used in the 1991 GHS survey of 'childcare for children under five' make it impossible to calculate how many children attended each of the main types of provision. Over the whole 0-4 age range, the most common form of provision is playgroups; playgroups provide for more children than all forms of school combined (an estimated 890,000 versus 758,000 pupils in maintained and private schools). However as a substantial proportion of children at playgroup are under 3 (nearly a fifth in 1986, mainly 2-year-olds), while there are very few 2-year-olds in school, there may be slightly more children in the age group 3-4 attending school than playgroup.

★ By international standards, *compulsory schooling begins at an early age* in Britain. Most children start primary school even younger due to early admission to reception class - with the exception of Scotland where relatively few 4-year-olds are in reception class. The only other countries to admit children early to primary schools are Ireland and Netherlands (where in fact the first two years of primary school were originally separate nursery classes for 4- and 5-year-olds; now children start compulsory schooling at 5, but can attend from 4).

★ *Only 52% of children attending 'schools' in Britain are at maintained nursery education*; the rest are in reception class (42%) or private schools (6%). Put another way, in 1991, 51% of 3- and 4-year-olds were at school, but 3% were in private schools and 21% in reception class in primary school, leaving 26% in nursery education. As most of the children attending maintained nursery schooling go part-time, on a full-time equivalent basis there were *places* in nursery education for only 15% of 3- and 4-year-olds. By contrast, places for over 3s in most other countries are overwhelmingly in nursery education (or kindergartens) and mostly provided on a full-time basis. *The UK is unique in depending so heavily in its provision for children over 3 on playgroups, early admission to primary school and a 'shift system' for nursery education.*

★ Where children do receive nursery education in Britain, they mostly *attend for only a year*; elsewhere, nursery education (or kindergarten) is normally attended for 3 years.

3. An annotated table of participation in 'early childhood care and education services' for children between 3 and 5

For reasons explained above, it is impossible to provide comparative material on services for children under 3. Their exclusion below should be read in this light, and is extremely unsatisfactory. It leaves a very partial picture of 'early childhood care and education services'.

---

2 These playgroup figures come from the PPA's annual survey of its members and apply to sessional playgroups, which account for over 80% of playgroups where children can be left by their carers. The proportion of children per place is similar or even higher in playgroups offering longer hours (PPA, 1993)

I have concentrated on providing data on attendance at 'early childhood care and education services' for children *aged 3 to 5*; these services include kindergartens, day nurseries, family daycare and playgroups, as well as schools. The statistics are however limited in two ways:

(i) They cover services that are mainly or wholly *publicly funded*, because there are no comparable statistics in most countries for other services (for example, for children attending private nurseries, playgroups or childminders). For reasons outlined above, it can be argued that the availability of these services is particularly important. Even limited to publicly funded services, there are still some gaps.

(ii) They are confined to a number of *European countries*, mainly Member States of the EU and Nordic countries.

Adopting this approach enhances Britain's position in the Table in two ways. First, because it is a count of *children attending*, it includes the many British children attending schools on a part-time basis; a league table based on a count of full-time equivalent *places* would have shown Britain in a less favourable light. Second, because it is a count of the 3-5 age range, all 5-year-olds are included as attending a service because of compulsory schooling; a league table based on children attending services between 3 and the start of compulsory schooling would again have shown the UK less favourably. However, it should also be noted that the approach adopted, with its criterion of public funding, excludes playgroups, which provide a service (generally of very limited hours and of a very under-resourced nature) for most children not attending school, as well as those children attending private and unsubsidised day nurseries and childminders.

I have presented two sets of data:

(i) *the proportion of children aged 3-5 (i.e.a three year age range) attending services.* I have based this on two sources: first, Table 12 from the recent OECD (1993) review of early childhood education; second, various national sources, where I can fill gaps in the OECD table. These gaps occur because the OECD review presents no data at all for some countries (eg.Greece, Italy, Luxembourg) and has problems with definitions for the Nordic countries. I have included both services in 'schools' and in other publicly funded services (for example, the range of centre-based services provided in Nordic countries). I have also used national data for 'unified' Germany, rather than referring only to the former West Germany, as in the OECD review.

(ii) the proportion of children aged 3, 4 and 5 attending services.

The Table below refers to 1991 (unless otherwise stated). A full explanation is given in the notes for each country, which are provided after the Table *and which should always be consulted before interpreting the statistics contained in the Table.*

Table 1.   *International comparisons of compulsory school age and % of children attending publicly funded services.*

	Compulsory school age	% of children attending publicly funded services aged (years):			
		3	4	5	3-5
Belgium (1991)	6	97	99	98	98
Denmark (1992)	7	76	81	79	79
Finland (1992)	7	44	49	53	60
France (1991)	6	98	101	99	99
Germany (1990)	6	-	-	-	77
Greece (1991)	5.5	-	-	CS	88(*)
Ireland (1991)	6	1(+)	55(+)	98	51(+*)
Italy (1992)	6	-	-	-	91
Luxembourg (1990)	5	7	95	CS	67(*)
Netherlands (1991)	5	(+)	98	CS	67(*)
Norway (1992)	7	49	60	68	53
Portugal (1991)	6	28	44	63	45
Spain (1991)	6	28	94	100	74
Sweden (1992)	7	63	67	75	68
Britain (1991)	5	41(+)	58(+)	CS	65(+*)

CS *indicates where 5-year-olds are covered wholly or partly by compulsory schooling (and in these cases, a 100% attendance level for 5-year-olds is included in the '3-5' column);*
+   *indicates that a source of publicly-funded provision is not included, because data is not available;*
*   *indicates that a substantial qualification exists concerning the statistic for the whole 3-5 age range.*

Notes on Table

Belgium   *Source:* OECD

★   Children can start nursery education from 2.5 years. Nearly a quarter of 2-year-olds (22%) attend.

★   Nursery schooling is usually attended on a full time basis, that is for about 7 hours a day (except for Wednesday afternoon, when schools are closed).

Denmark   *Source:* Annual census of welfare institutions, Danmarks Statistik

★   The figures cover a range of services, which are the responsibility of 'social welfare' authorities (though provided by a mix of public and private agencies). These services combine a care and pedagogical role and include kindergartens (which account for 61% of children), age-integrated centres (26%), other centres (2%) and organised family daycare (10%).

★   Nearly all 6-year-olds and some 5-year-olds attend a 'kindergarten class' in primary school for 3-4 hours a day; unlike other services for children under 7, these classes are the responsibility of education authorities and are intended to make the transition to school easier. The figure of 75% is therefore probably a good estimate for attendance by children aged 3-5.

★   While 'kindergarten class' hours are short (3-4 hours), other services for children below compulsory school age are generally open for 10 hours a day, and children attend on average for 7 hours a day.

★   Denmark also has high attendance levels at publicly funded services for children under 3 – about 49% – and is the only country in the EC where most under 3s attend publicly funded services. Denmark is also unusual in having an integrated service for children under compulsory school age, with a common, high level (3.5 years) basic training for staff working with children from 0-6.

★   The Government has recently made a commitment to meet the demand for services for children from 0-6.

Finland   *Source:* Personal communication from the Ministry of Social Affairs and Health

★   The figure for children aged 3-5 includes 19% in organised family day care and 29% in centres.

★   In addition to the figures shown in the Table, a further 11% of children attend other services including 'open centres' (mainly for mothers who are at home and their children) and centres for children with special needs.

★   Compulsory schooling does not start until 7; 67% of children aged 6 attend some form of publicly-funded service.

France   *Source:* OECD

★   Children can start nursery education from 2 years. Over a third of 2-year-olds (35%) attend.

★   Nursery schooling is usually attended on a full time basis, that is for about 8 hours a day (except for Wednesday afternoon, when schools are closed).

Germany   *Source:* Personal communication from Federal Government

★   At the time of unification, the former West Germany had kindergarten places for nearly 70% of children, compared to 95% in the former East Germany. There was an even larger difference for publicly funded services for children under 3.

★   In the former East Germany, kindergartens are usually open all day (i.e.10-12 hours). In the former West Germany, only about 14% of places are open for the full day; the rest are usually open for 4 hours in the morning and, in some cases, for 2 hours in the afternoon.

★   The Government has recently made a commitment to provide kindergarten places for all children aged 3-6 by 1996.

Greece   *Source:* Bairrao and Tietze (1993)

★   There is a divided system. The education authorities provide nursery classes for children from 3.5 years, which are open for 4 hours a day. The Ministry of Health provides kindergartens, which take children from 2.5 years and are open 9 hours a day. Children start primary school at 5.5.

★   The '3-5' figure in the Table of 88% (64% for nursery classes, 25% for kindergartens) is for children aged 3.5 to 5.5 (i.e.it covers only 2 of the 3 years). All children between 5.5 and 6 will be at school; on the other hand, only a minority of children between 3 and 3.5 will attend publicly funded services because nursery classes are not available to this age group. Taking both of these into account, therefore, the actual '3-5' figure might be between 75% and 80%.

Ireland   *Source:* OECD

★ There is no nursery education in Ireland. The figures in the Table are for children admitted to Primary School before compulsory schooling which starts at 6.

★ *In addition to the figures in the Table,* some children receive public funding at other services; however, the number is small, and unlikely to increase the figures given in the Table by more than 2-3%.

★ The main form of provision for children from 2.5 to 4 years is playgroups. Most children only attend for 5-6 hours a week, and most playgroups receive no public funds; those that do mainly receive only small sums of money.

Italy   *Source:* INSEE

★ There is a widespread system of publicly funded nursery education, but provided by a variety of agencies: national government (53% of places), local authorities (13%), other public organisations (6%) and private organisations (including religious bodies) (27%).

★ Schools provided by national government are required to be open at least 8 hours a day, and may be open as long as 10 hours a day. About 70% of all children attending nursery schools do so for more than 7 hours a day.

Luxembourg   *Source:* EC Childcare Network (1990)

★ Nearly all 4-year-olds attend nursery education, which is open 6 hours a day on three days per week and 3.5-4 hours a day on three days (including Saturday). Compulsory schooling starts at 5.

★ There is no nursery schooling for 3-year-olds. However there are places for about 7% of 3-4 year-olds in publicly-funded centres, providing full-time care for 3-year-olds and out-of-school care for 4-year-olds.

Netherlands   *Source:* OECD, EC Childcare Network (1990), Bairrao and Tietze (1993)

★ Nearly all 4-year-olds attend primary school, although this is on a voluntary basis. Compulsory schooling starts at 5.

★ There is no nursery schooling for 3-year-olds. A large number of 2- and 3-year-olds (about a half altogether) go to playgroups. However, children only attend on average for 5-6 hours a week. Nearly all playgroups receive some public funds, which cover nearly half their costs.

★ *In addition to the figures in the Table,* there has been a substantial increase in centres providing full-time care for children from 0-3 (plus out-of-school care for children aged 4 and over), as the result of a Government Initiative. In 1989, there were 16,000 places; in 1994 there will be 60,000. Approximately a third of the cost of these services comes from public funds. I have no information on the number of places available in these services for 3-year-olds.

★ If playgroups and other centres receiving public funds were included, then the figure for the '3-5' range would be over 80%. However, a significant proportion of this figure would come from services providing very short hours (playgroups) and receiving limited public funding (i.e.covering half or less of their costs).

Norway   *Source:* Personal communication, Royal Ministry of Children and Family Affairs.

★ The percentage is for children attending centres.

★ Hours of opening of centres vary; in 1992 77% of centres were open more than 30 hours a week. Nearly two-thirds (62%) of children aged 1-6 years attending centres went for more than 30 hours a week.

★ Compulsory schooling does not start until 7; 84% of children aged 6 attend some form of publicly-funded service.

★ The Government is committed to meeting the demand for services by the year 2000.

Portugal   *Source:* OECD

★ There is a divided system. The education authorities provide nursery schools for children from 3 years, which are open for 6-7 hours a day. The Ministry of Health has responsibility for kindergartens, many of which are provided by private organisations, and which are open for up to 11 hours a day. Kindergartens are mostly organised to support employed mothers.

★ Portugal has the second highest maternal employment rate in the EU (after Denmark). Given the relatively limited provision of publicly funded services and the high level of parental employment, many parents will need to use private services or informal arrangements (relatives etc.) for 3-5 year-olds.

Spain   *Source:* OECD

* Some nursery schooling is provided privately and parents pay the full fees. In the near future, it is expected that most of this schooling will be funded by public money but continue to be operated by private organisations.

* Nursery schools are generally open for 8 hours, with a long lunch break.

* The Government is committed to provide nursery education places for all children aged 3-6 by 1996.

Sweden   *Source:* Personal communication from the Ministry of Health and Social Affairs

* The figures include children attending centres and family daycare, most on a full-time basis, as well as some children attending part-time groups (*deltidsgrupper*) for 4-6 year olds who are cared for at home or by family day carers.

* Sweden is in the process of lowering the school age to 6. At present, all 6-year-olds are entitled to attend full-time centres or part-time groups for at least 525 hours in the year.

Britain   *Source:* OECD (1993), DfE (1992), Scottish Office (1992), Welsh Office (1992)

* The '3-5' figure is for children in maintained schools (3% has been removed from the OECD statistics to take account of children in private schools). It is made up of 26% of 3- and 4-year-olds in nursery schooling; 21% of 3- and 4-year-olds in reception class; and 100% of 5-year-olds in primary school. A large proportion of children receiving nursery schooling (88%) attend on a part-time basis of 2.5 hours per day. Most children in reception class and primary school attend for a full school day.

* A large number of 3- and 4-year-olds attend playgroups (40% of the age group in 1986). Attendance at playgroup is, on average, for 6 hours a week. In 1993, less than half (46%) received any external financial assistance (from public funds or other sources), and the grant received by these playgroups was, on average, equivalent to 25% of average annual expenditure. So, although a few playgroups in local authorities with an active funding policy receive most of their income from public funds, the great majority depend largely or wholly on private sources of income (fees and fundraising).

* *In addition to the figures given in the Table,* official statistics show that about 1.5% of children aged 0-4 attend either publicly funded day nurseries or have their fees paid at private services from public funds; there is no information about whether this proportion is constant across the 0-4 age range or whether more or less 3- and 4-year-olds are publicly funded in this way. These official statistics may however underestimate the number of children whose placements are publicly subsidised. A generous estimate might add a further 5% to the number of 3- and 4-year-olds in publicly funded services, raising the figure for the '3-5' range by some 3% to 68%.

References

Bairrao, J. and Tietze, W. (1993) *Early Childhood Services in the European Community: Recommendations for Progress,* report prepared for the European Commission Task Force on Human Resources, Education, Training and Youth.

Balaguer, I. (1993) 'LOGSE: a new direction in services for young children', in *Employment, Equality and Caring for Children (1992 Annual Report of the EC Network on Childcare and Other Measures to reconcile Employment and Family Responsibilities),* Brussels: European Commission (DGV)

Bridgwood, A. and Savage, D. (1993) *General Household Survey, 1991,* London: HMSO

Department for Education (1992) *Pupils under Five Years of Age in Schools in England - January 1991 (Statistical Bulletin 11/92),* London: DfE

European Commission Childcare Network (1990) *Childcare in the European Communities (Women of Europe Supplement No.31),* Brussels: European Commission (Women's Information Service)

Government Statistical Service (1993) *Education Statistics for the UK; 1992 Edition,* London: HMSO

OECD (1993) *Education at a Glance: OECD Indicators,* Paris: OECD

OPCS (1989) *General Household Survey, 1986,* London: HMSO

Pre-school Playgroups Association (1993) *Facts and Figures 1993,* London: PPA

Scottish Office (1992) *Provision for Pre-school Children (Statistical Bulletin, Education Series, Edn/A2/1992/11),* Edinburgh: Scottish Office

Welsh Office (1992) *Statistics of Education in Wales: Schools (No.5 1991),* Cardiff: Welsh Office

APPENDIX G

A Good Start in Education

This is reproduced by kind permission of the National Commission on Education: from *Learning to Succeed: A Radical Look at Education Today and A Strategy for the Future*. Report of the Paul Hamlyn Foundation National Commission on Education, Heinemann, November 1993, £4.99. *Learning to Succeed* can be obtained through bookshops or by writing to: Special Sales Department, Reed Book Services Limited, Northampton Road, Rushden, Northants, NN10 9RZ.

Introduction

Throughout the United Kingdom there are wide variations in provision for children below compulsory school age. Some pre-school services have explicit educational aims, while others are concerned mainly with daycare, and some offer a combination of daycare and education. Some children are taught free of charge by trained teachers in nursery schools or classes. Others attend playgroups or nurseries for which their parents pay, and many are in the care of paid childminders. Children needing specialist help may be in day nurseries run by social services departments. A minority has no experience of pre-school groups of any kind outside the home. This diversity does not mean effective choice for parents, still less the guarantee of high quality educational experience for young children.

How important is it for children to receive education before they reach compulsory school age? It may be argued that, when resources are in short supply, we should concentrate public funds on compulsory schooling and on education and training to equip young people for work. Indeed, the view of the Department for Education is that school-age children should have priority, and that the extent and nature of provision for younger children is a matter for local authorities and schools to decide.(1)

That view ignores the significance of the first five years of a child's life in preparing 'the foundation for all skills and later learning'.(2) In these early years a high percentage of children's learning takes place. They grow in their physical competence, in their knowledge of how the world works, and in their skills for getting on with others. It is a time when children establish attitudes and behaviour patterns which are vital for future learning progress and social development. They also begin to develop a sense of self, and of self-esteem, which helps educational achievement later.(3) Thus, by confining attention solely to compulsory education, opportunities to increase attainment are neglected.

Children do not begin schools with equal chances of benefiting from it. It is estimated that just under a third of under-5s – a higher proportion than of all children – live in households with less than 50% of the national average income.(4) Poverty and the associated problems of poor housing, inadequate nutrition and ill-health create stressful conditions for parents raising families and can jeopardise children's success in school. Over 20% of young people in some poor urban areas in England leave school without qualifications, compared with about 9% in the country as a whole.

Educational achievement is strongly associated with family background. Parental education, particularly the level of education achieved by the mother, has a powerful influence on children's educational progress. When the mother herself has not had the benefit of a good education or learned to recognise its value, there is a risk that her child's early learning experience will be impoverished unless there is outside help.

Our society is becoming increasingly multicultural. For many schoolchildren English is not the language spoken at home. This is true of more than a quarter of 7-year-olds in Bradford, for example. Results from the national tests of 7-year-olds revealed, not surprisingly, that such children tended to perform less well than those whose mother tongue was English. Pre-school education which helps ethnic minority children to develop their English language skills will therefore have positive benefits.

Even at the beginning of the infant school stage, differences in children's skills are apparent and these differences tend to persist throughout primary schooling and beyond. Indeed, studies show that pupils' early attainment at school is a good indicator of later educational success, and perhaps a more reliable indicator than family background.(5) This underlines the importance of encouraging success from the earliest possible moment.

It is essential that when children start school they are ready to take advantage of what school has to offer. Pre-school education alone cannot ensure that, but it can make a significant difference. If we are determined to seek every worthwhile opportunity to improve children's chances of learning to succeed, the potential offered by good early childhood education must be seized.

This chapter examines the case for greater investment in high-quality provision for under-5s. We consider the evidence on the effects of pre-school provision, and go on to discuss the demand created by changes in the family, in employment patterns and in social condition. Next we review the extent and quality of present arrangements. We conclude with recommendations for expansion and improvement. Our main concern is with educational services rather than daycare, though we argue that the two cannot be separated.

Effects of early childhood education

Those who wish to expand and improve pre-school education are under pressure to justify any claims for increased resources by demonstrating that better services will result in measurable long-term benefits. This is a difficult proposition since any benefits which a child experiences as a result of attending a nursery class or playgroup will clearly be affected by subsequent experience in school. For example, nursery provision may advance children's language development, but the extent to which this progress is sustained will be influenced by the quality of language teaching at primary school. A specially-designed and well-controlled longitudinal research project would be required in order to provide reliable evidence, and such a study has not yet been carried out in this country.

The research which has already been undertaken, supported by informed opinion, does provide convincing evidence of the beneficial impact which good pre-school services can have on young children's learning and social behaviour. Studies in the USA and in the UK have amply demonstrated this potential. A summary of some important indicators is offered here.

A large-scale study which examined the relationship between children's pre-school experiences and their attainment at 5 and 10 years of age reported marked differences in ability, attainment and behaviour at age 10 between those who had attended pre-school groups and those who had not.(6) The authors concluded that children from small home-based playgroups (in predominantly middle-class areas) and children from nursery schools did particularly well.

A small study of working-class children during their first year in primary school reported that 'graduates' of well-resourced local authority nursery education showed certain advantages in their ability to settle into school, compared with children who had attended poorly resourced playgroups.(7) Children from nursery classes were more likely to play in a purposeful and creative way, to persevere when they encountered difficulties in their school work, to engage in connected conversation, and to show greater motivation for school, spending more time on 'academic' tasks.

One researcher in Britain has pioneered highly structured enrichment programmes for pre-school children, demonstrating that it is possible to reduce the gap between the academic performance of disadvantaged and advantaged pupils.(8) This study also suggests that parental involvement in pre-school education can have beneficial effects on the younger siblings of the child receiving education.

In the United States, a review of a wide range of pre-school programmes concluded that early intervention to provide for the children of low income families can have measured effects throughout childhood and into adolescence.(9) Children who had participated in pre-school programmes were more likely to succeed in school, showed better self-esteem, had more realistic vocational expectations and were prouder of their achievements. Important features of these projects were that they were all carefully designed and well-supported, with high ratios of adults to children and active parental involvement.

An American programme known as the High/Scope Perry Preschool Project has attracted considerable attention in the UK, due in part to the striking cost/benefit claims which have been made.(10) High/Scope was a high-quality, active learning pre-school programme which concentrated on guided play. Adults encouraged and supported children in planning and reviewing their own activities, helping them to develop persistence and to believe in their talents.

The project has followed the lives of 123 children from disadvantaged African American families, comparing those who took part in the pre-school programme with a control group of children who stayed at home. The participants were regularly assessed during childhood and into adulthood, most recently at age 27.

Throughout their school years, the High/Scope children did better than their peers who had not attended the nursery programme, spent less time in remedial classes and were more likely to have completed school or training. As adults, they were more likely to have jobs, to own homes, and to be higher paid, and were less likely to have received social services assistance or to have been involved in crime. It has been calculated that for every dollar invested in the children who attended the programme, $7.16 (after controlling for inflation) is returned to the tax-payer by way of savings on the costs of juvenile delinquency, remedial education, income support and joblessness.

The case for investment in early education rather than reliance on remedial programmes has been made in England by the Family Policy Studies Centre.(11) It argues in a recent report that pre-school provision, by giving children an educational 'head start', encourages school success and thereby makes an important contribution to reducing the danger that children will be attracted to delinquent peer groups and criminal activities.

Effects of daycare

Many under-5s in the UK are placed in centres or nurseries which are predominantly concerned with daycare rather than education, and children of working parents often experience a mixture of both.

Where there are above average levels of daycare, where the quality of the care is high, or where the children come from a mixed social background, there have been positive results.(12) In Sweden for instance, where local authority nurseries are available to families from all walks of life, it has emerged that daycare experience can give children a better start in school. In the USA, it has been found that children who attend high-quality nurseries subsequently perform well in educational and social assessments at school. Encouraging evidence also comes from a study in Manchester.(13) There, levels of daycare are above average, and daycare children are reported to be socially and intellectually ahead of children who do not have this experience.

In one UK study daycare children performed less well towards the end of primary school compared with other children. This result must be qualified by the observation that publicly-funded daycare in the UK is usually highly selective, concentrating on children from families known to be in need, who require a high degree of support which daycare staff may not always be well-qualified to give. We should also ask whether the quality of the curriculum offered in daycare centres and nurseries is high enough. A recent study found that staff in nurseries run by social services were less well-equipped to provide a high-quality nursery curriculum than teachers in the education sector.(14)

Changing employment patterns and social conditions

The potential advantages to later learning form an important aspect of the case for good early years provision. Many parents, however, would see the issue in far more immediate terms. For them, financial need, the demands of work and the daily stresses of family life loom large. Social and employment conditions have changed, creating new needs and expectations.

The growth of two-earner households, the rise in the proportion of children living in single-parent families, and the increase in family breakdown and divorce all have a bearing on the quality of children's lives. Children in remote rural areas as well as those living in high-rise flats in urban areas suffer from isolation, lacking social contact and safe places to play. This led a parliamentary committee in 1988 to say that the case for under-5s provision should not be put solely in terms of longer-term benefits.(15) Pre-school education 'is not merely a preparation for something else, but caters for the child's needs at that time and may be justified in those terms'.

Women's participation in the labour market is growing. In future, women's employment patterns will resemble those of men far more closely than in the past. Already women account for 49% of employees in the UK. Employment rates for women with a child under 5 are rising: 43% in Great Britain were in full- or part-time work in 1991 compared with 35% in 1987 and 30% in 1985. It is estimated that 48% of women in Great Britain with children under 5 will be in employment by 2001.(16) With improvements in daycare provision and greater flexibility of working hours, and assuming an expansion in the national economy to allow more women to work, this rate could increase to 65%.(17)

For lone mothers, employment rates are lower, though the need for paid work is arguably greater. The rate of full-time employment among lone mothers with a child under 5 in the UK is the lowest in the EC. Surveys suggest that many non-working mothers would like to take up employment if suitable, affordable child care could be found.

Child poverty is associated with mothers not working. In 1988-9, dependent children in single parent families without work were over-represented among those in the bottom 20% of the income distribution, accounting for 29%. In the child population as a whole, approximately 18% were estimated to live in single-parent families in 1991, compared with 11.4% in 1981.

It is claimed in a recent study that analysis of the costs and benefits of expanded public child care shows that there would be economic benefits to the Exchequer resulting from tax paid by women working, and from a reduction in the dependence of families on state benefits.(18) There would be potential to generate new income (with tax flowbacks) from extra jobs in child care. In addition, it is suggested that women's pay and career opportunities would be enhanced: their loss of earnings from time spent caring for children would be smaller, and increased work experience would give them access to higher incomes.

Major employers are now calling for 'a national strategy for accessible, available, affordable, quality child care' on the grounds that this would help companies to be competitive in world markets and prevent wastage of resources invested in the training of female employees who are unable to continue their careers after the birth of their children.(19)

What the evidence tells us

The Commission draws the following conclusions from its review of research and other evidence:

1   To make an effective contribution to children's later learning and behaviour, and reduce the need for remedial work, early childhood education and care services must be of high quality: well-resourced, with appropriately trained staff and suitable adult to child ratios.

2   A high-quality nursery curriculum is one which enables children to enter school with a positive out-look, by developing self-esteem, commitment to learning, and a belief that if they try, they can succeed. The curriculum should value and give expression to children's different cultural backgrounds. It should encourage all children's language development, paying particular attention to the needs of those whose mother tongue is not English.

3   Early childhood programmes are more likely to succeed where there is effective parental involvement. This does not mean that involving parents can be an alternative to employing sufficient numbers of highly qualified professionals. Nor does it imply that all parents will be willing or able to accept the same degree of involvement. The message we wish to convey is that pre-school programmes create opportunities for professionals to support parents in their role as 'first educators' of their children, and to establish from a very early stage the idea of parent-professional partnership based on mutual respect and a shared purpose.

4   Good pre-school programmes can be particularly beneficial for children from disadvantaged backgrounds and for those over the age of 3.

5   There is value in developing services which cater for all children, rather than segregating and hence stigmatising children from the neediest families.

6   Good pre-school services will help to reduce the stress on families and children, particularly those living on low incomes, and contributing to lifting children out of poverty by enabling mothers to work.

7   As part of wider employment and social policies, good pre-school education and affordable child care will help parents to reconcile the demands of responsible parenting and work outside the home.

8   Better provision for under-5s will yield benefits for the economy.

Under-5s provision in the UK

We illustrate five aspects of provision for under-5s, concentrating mainly on educational provision in maintained nursery and primary schools:

*   growth in participation;
*   the uneven spread of provision;
*   the different treatment of 3- and 4-year-olds;
*   4-year-olds in infant classes;
*   the diversity of providers.

Growth in participation

There has been a substantial increase since 1980-81 in the number of pupils under 5 attending all types of school (both maintained and independent) in the UK, as Table 6.1 shows.(20) Overall, the numbers have increased by 39%. This represents a growth in participation of 8.5 percentage points, mostly attributable to part-time attendance. About 50% of 3- and 4-year-olds attended school in 1990-91.

Table 6.1 Pupils aged under 5 attending all types of school, 1980-81 and 1990-91, United Kingdom

All pupils aged under 5	1980-81 (Thousand)	1990-91 (Thousand)	Increase
Mode of attendance			
Full-time	326	406	+25%
Part-time	247	394	+60%
All pupils	573	799	+39%
Participation rate	44.3%	52.8%	+8.5%

Source: Government Statistical Service.(20)

Uneven spread of provision

It is important to note that Northern Ireland differs from the rest of the United Kingdom in having a compulsory school age of 4 rather than 5. Children who reach the age of 4 by 1 July start school in the following September, a policy which was introduced from 1990-91. In Scotland, children who reach the age of 5 by the last day of February are required to start school in the previous August. Elsewhere in the UK, children are not legally required to attend school until the term following their fifth birthday.

Publicly-funded provision for under-5s is unevenly spread in the United Kingdom, as Table 6.2 illustrates. In Wales, 68% of under 5s were receiving education in 1992, compared with 49% in England. More than a third of under-5s in Wales and Scotland were in nursery schools and classes, compared with a quarter in England. The percentage of under-5s taught in infant classes ranged from 32% in Wales and Northern Ireland to 7% in Scotland.

Table 6.2   All pupils under 5 in public sector schools, 1991-2.

Percentage of 3- and 4-year-olds

	Nursery schools and nursery classes	Infant classes	Total
England	26%	23%	49%
Wales	36%	32%	68%
Scotland	34%	7%	41%
N. Ireland	15%	32%	47%

Sources: See note. (21)

There are also variations within countries.(22) For example, in all but one Welsh authority over 50% of 3- and 4-year-olds received education, while in England the percentage of under-5s in nursery and primary schools ranged from under 20% in three authorities (Bromley, West Sussex and Wiltshire) to over 80% in six authorities, including five metropolitan areas. In two English authorities – Cleveland and Walsall – over 90% of under-5s received education.

Different treatment of 3- and 4-year-olds

Of particular interest is the differing nature of provision made for 3- and 4-year-olds, shown in Table 6.3. Here, Northern Ireland's compulsory school age of 4 rather than 5 must be borne in mind.

Table 6.3   Three- and four-year-olds in public sector schools, 1992.

	Population		Pupils in nursery schools and nursery classes and participation rate				Pupils in infant classes in primary schools and participation rate			
	Aged 3 *Thousand*	Aged 4 *Thousand*	Aged 3 *Thousand*	%	Aged 4 *Thousand*	%	Aged 3 *Thousand*	%	Aged 4 *Thousand*	%
England	655	632	247	37.7	55	8.7	1	0.2	299	47.3
Wales	39	39	16	41.6	10	25.3	1	3.7	24	62.1
Scotland	67	65	12	18.6	32	49.2	0	0	9	14.5
N. Ireland	26	26	4	15.0	4	14.8	0	0	17	63.1

Sources: See note. (23)

In England, more than a third (38%) of 3-year-olds were receiving education, the vast majority in nursery rather than in primary provision. Over 50% of 4-year-olds were receiving education, but most of these were placed in infant classes in primary schools, normally on a full-time basis. This type of provision may not always be suitable for such young children, as we indicate in the next section of the chapter. Scotland presented a different pattern, with 49% of 4-year-olds in nursery schools and classes, and under 15% in infant classes. In Scotland and Northern Ireland, under 20% of 3-year-olds received education.

In the case of England, there were marked contrasts in the patterns of provision adopted by local authorities.(24) For example, Gloucestershire had no nursery schools or nursery classes, but admitted 94% of rising 5s and younger 4-year-olds to infant classes in primary schools. Birmingham admitted 97% of 4-year-olds to infant classes, but also catered for substantial numbers of 3-year-olds in nursery schools and classes. In Hillingdon only 5% of 4-year-olds entered infant classes; overall, 50% of under-5s were in pre-school provision, the majority in nursery classes.

Four-year-olds in infant classes

Growing parental demand for under-5s provision, combined with a shortage of nursery education places, and the availability of spare capacity in primary schools, has led to many children being admitted early to primary school, sometimes a year before they reach statutory school age. Early admission has become widespread in England and Wales, with only a minority of the age group attending nursery schools and classes.

Compulsory schooling in the UK starts earlier than in many other European countries. In France, Italy and Belgium, children start at age 6, in Germany between 6 and 7, and in Denmark at 7. One researcher warned in 1989 that in this country: 'if present trends continue, it will not be many years before virtually all children enter primary school before they are 5. The age of starting school will have become 4, in practice if not in statute.' (25) As we have noted, it is now statutory in Northern Ireland for children to start school at age 4.

It has been recognised that provision in infant classes can have serious drawbacks for 4-year-olds. The worry is that 'classroom organisation, curriculum objectives and teaching styles designed with one age group in mind are being applied to children up to a year younger'.(26) To this might be added unsuitable class sizes, inappropriate ratios of adults to children in the classroom, and an over-long school day. Indeed, local authority inspectors and advisers in England argued in evidence to a Parliamentary Select Committee in 1988 that it could be harmful to impose on 4-year-olds a curriculum designed for 5- and 6-year-olds.

The situation is different in Northern Ireland. Given the earlier compulsory school age, the national curriculum for the first year of primary school is designed to meet the developmental needs of 4-year-olds, concentrating on learning through experience and emphasising play. There are, however, concerns about the appropriateness of the provision made in primary classes for 4-year-olds who have not yet reached compulsory school age in September but join a class of more experienced pupils later in the year.

When HM Inspectors surveyed nursery and primary schools in England in the mid-1980s, they concluded that nursery schools and classes generally offered a broader, better balanced education for under-5s than infant classes.(27) Only a small number of the infant classes in their survey demonstrated work that was well-suited to under-5s; in most, the curriculum was not sufficiently matched to their educational needs.

The initial training of teachers in reception classes in England is a cause for concern, No up-to-date national information is published, but we note that a survey released in 1990 showed that only 12% of a sample of these teachers had initial training relating to under-5s.(28) Forty per cent were trained for age groups over the age of 7.

Some improvements are becoming apparent as a result of efforts by LEA early years advisers and teachers to adapt the curriculum and teaching methods to the needs of 4-year-olds. In a report on standards in education in 1990-91, HMI stated that in primary school reception and mixed-age classes, 'the standards of work and the curriculum for 4-year-olds ranged from good to poor but in general were better matched to pupils' needs than in previous years'.(29) Fears that the introduction of the national curriculum would result in 'the force-feeding of under-5s with inappropriate work' have proved unfounded, according to the inspectors. They believe that the national curriculum is exerting a beneficial effect: as early years teachers now have more certain knowledge of what will be taught in the first stage of the national curriculum, they are better able to plan a balanced programme for under-5s.

The ratio of adults to children is improving in some schools, where, for example, schools have used the freedom offered by local management to recruit non-teaching assistants and are deploying them to work with the youngest children.

It is vital that when children begin schooling it should not be a distressing and alienating experience. Even for those who have had the benefit of pre-school provision, starting school can prove daunting, and studies have found that between 13% and 15% of children have difficulties in adjusting.(30) More provision for under-5s does not necessarily mean better provision; improvements in quantity need to be combined with greater quality. Attention must be given to ensuring that, when they enter school, children are ready to benefit from the more formal structure it offers.

Information was not available to enable the Commission to reach a comprehensive and accurate judgement about the quality of provision for 4-year-olds in infant classes. A new survey by HMI on standards in reception classes (which some schools provided for children admitted before the age of 5) was awaited when we completed our report.

A diversity of providers

We have so far concentrated chiefly on provision for under-5s in maintained nursery and primary schools. However, a key feature of present arrangements is the great diversity of agencies in the maintained, private and voluntary sectors offering different kinds of services, some educational, some primarily concerned with daycare, and some combining the two. Briefing No. 8 for the Commission outlines the five major categories: nursery education (including nursery schools and nursery classes in primary schools); reception classes which admit children under compulsory school age; day nurseries; playgroups; and childminders.(31) Within the range there is a mixture of public and private provision.

The huge increase in private services - private nurseries, playgroups and childminders - is evident from Table 6.4. The largest category, in terms of the number of places, is that of playgroups. Parents' ability to pay is clearly a strong determining factor in the kind of early education and care which children receive. It is important to note that most playgroups offer approximately two sessions (a total of five hours) per week, whereas most nursery education takes up two and a half hours per day. With regard not only to the balance of public and private provision, but also to the number of hours offered, the UK may be thought to compare unfavourably with other EC countries, offering publicly-funded provision for less than

50% of children between the age of 3 and the start of compulsory schooling. This contrasts sharply with over 95% in France and Belgium, 85% in Denmark and Italy; and 77% in Germany.

Table 6.4   *Number of places in early childhood care and education provision, 1980, 1991, England.*

Types of provision	1980	1991	% change 1980-1991
Nursery education	130,997	177,863	+36
Reception class	205,673	272,178	+32
Local authority day nurseries	28,437	27,039	-5
Private nurseries	22,017	79,029	+259
Playgroups	367,868	428,420	+16
Childminders	98,495	233,258	+137

Source: Sylva K. and Moss P., November 1992. (32)

We recognise that the picture of educational provision for under-5s is not static. For example, following the May 1993 county council elections some new councils are adopting policies to extend or improve their nursery education provision. Our review of the available data indicates, however, that there are insufficient high-quality nursery education places for 3- and 4-year-olds to meet the demands of the next century. Though there is diversity, there is unequal access and limited effective choice for parents. While we acknowledge that the quality of what is offered to 4-year-olds in primary schools in England is improving, it is important to register the weight of concern expressed in evidence to the Commission that much provision for this age group remains inappropriate.

How much does present provision need to improve?

Several reports have attempted to gauge the shortfall in provision of education and care services. There are many difficulties in assessing the volume of unmet demand for different types of services and it is unlikely that this can be predicted accurately. Research for the National Children's Bureau has concluded that a mixture of provision will continue to be required: a choice of educational provision as between nursery schools/classes and playgroups, and also a mix of care and education.(33) For example, by concentrating solely on nursery education, we would risk neglecting the most disadvantaged children, whose parents need ready access to a combination of daycare and education facilities.

In 1972, a Government White Paper (Education: A Framework for Expansion) recommended that educational provision should be sufficient to cater for 50% of 3-year-olds and 90% of 4-year-olds. Given the increase in demand for under-5s provision since that date, these figures might need to be revised upwards: the National Children's Bureau study suggests targets of 85% of 3-year-olds and 95% of 4-year-olds.

How do these targets compare with present levels of provision? As shown in Table 6.3, 38% of 3-year-olds and 56% of 4-year-olds in England were in maintained nursery and primary schools in 1992. A small percentage (around 4%) was in independent and special schools. Assuming no increase in this proportion, we would need to see provision for 3-year-olds in nursery and primary schools more than doubled, and that for 4-year-olds increased by two-thirds, if these targets are to be reached solely on the basis of the maintained sector.

There are indications that parents prefer pre-school settings with educational objectives. This does not imply an exclusive preference for nursery education in the form of nursery schools and classes: some diversity of provision seems more likely to meet parents' wishes. Playgroups represent a major proportion of all under-5s provision. Many are excellent, but quality within this sector is known to be highly variable, and concern has been expressed about under-resourcing, inadequate premises, lack of suitable equipment, insufficient training, and high staff turnover. If playgroups are improved – by employing more staff with suitable qualifications, offering greater local authority support, increasing the number of sessions for each child and making more places available free of charge – they are likely to meet part of the demand for nursery education.

We have noted that it is difficult to judge the amount of improvement needed in primary school provision for 4-year-old children who are below the compulsory age for starting school. A Parliamentary Committee recommended in 1988 that: 'no further steps be taken by LEAs towards introducing 3- and 4-year-olds into inappropriate primary school settings'.(34) The National Children's Bureau's study assumed limited expansion in primary school provision for under-5s to keep up with the expected increase in the number of children aged 3 and 4; the main expansion to meet demand would come from nursery schools and classes.(35) That report, like the Parliamentary report and that of the Committee of Inquiry which advised the DES in 1990,(36) called for current primary provision for 4-year-olds to be brought up to the standard of good nursery education.

Recommendations

High quality publicly-funded education provision should be available for all 3- and 4-year-olds. The opportunity for every child to learn to succeed right from the start should not rest on such factors as:

> where a child lives, when his or her birthday is, whether the parents have access to information about services and whether they can afford fees where there is no public provision.(37)

There is both demand and need for a diversity of early childhood services in the UK, with an emphasis on provision which offers a high-quality educational component specifically designed to meet the learning needs of children under compulsory school age, and with educational facilities well co-ordinated with daycare. Over a number of years, a consensus about the value of good pre-school provision has grown: action should now be taken to ensure that well rehearsed and desirable aims are put into practice as soon as possible.

Although we have concentrated on the needs of 3- and 4-year-olds as a matter of priority, we are aware that increasing numbers of children under the age of 3 are cared for away from home. Educational policies should also address their needs. Many special educational needs, for example, can be identified before the child is 3 years old. There is a case for regarding 0-5 as the first stage in our education system.

As to the type of educational provision we would advocate, the ideal would seem to be an expansion of nursery education based on nursery schools and nursery classes in primary schools. However, because of the wide variety and levels or provision existing in different parts of the UK, we favour a more pragmatic approach at this stage, taking account of the current state of provision in each local authority, whilst not compromising on quality. A range of providers could contribute to an expansion of nursery education, provided that they offer learning programmes of good quality which match the developmental needs of the children they serve.

A statutory nursery education service

This leads us to recommend a national strategy for improving early childhood education and care. A major component should be a statutory requirement on local authorities to ensure that sufficient high-quality, publicly-funded nursery education places are available for all 3-and 4-year olds whose parents wish it. Places should be offered on a half-time basis for 4-year-olds, though with reasonable flexibility to cater for children requiring shorter or less frequent periods of attendance. This goal can be achieved by developing a range of facilities in accordance with local circumstances, children's needs and parental preferences.

National standards

As a first step, national criteria should be devised to ensure that all facilities meet the educational standards of good nursery schools and classes. These should cover:

1 A curriculum for 3- and 4-year-olds, which we believe should be broadly defined and not unduly prescriptive.

2 The training and continuing professional development of education and care workers.

3 Teacher to pupil and adult to child ratios in all types of settings for the education and care of under-5s.

By 'curriculum' we do not imply an excessively formal school-based programme, but one which is geared to the needs of young children and emphasises first-hand experience and the central role of play and talk in learning and development.

We place particular emphasis on appropriate training. Whether in daycare facilities, playgroups, nursery schools and classes or in primary school infant classes, the education of children under compulsory school age should be the responsibility of staff with an appropriate early years education qualification. Teaching very young children is a complex task demanding a high level of skill and understanding. The Commission supports graduate-level training. We welcome the efforts now being made to establish a variety of routes to qualification, including higher level NVQs, and modular degrees specialising in early childhood study, which might be combined with teacher training. Consideration should also be given to incorporating a multiprofessional dimension in training, so that both childcare and education are covered.

Developing these standards and preparing advice on implementation for local managers and practitioners should be a task for the national authorities concerned with the curriculum and with teacher management, drawing on the guidelines already proposed by the Government's Committee of Inquiry into the quality of education for 3- and 4-year-olds.(38) Implementing and monitoring the standards should be a matter for local Education and Training Boards – the organisations which the Commission suggests establishing in the place of Local Education Authorities, and which we describe in Chapter 13.

Targets for improvement

National standards should be accompanied by targets for improvement. The Commission recommends the following:

★ within 5 years at most, nursery education places, meeting nationally agreed standards, for children in deprived areas within each local authority. We emphasise that this target should be seen as part of a wider plan to provide places for all children in the longer term, to avoid attaching social stigma to provision for the neediest children;

★ within the present decade, nursery education places, meeting nationally agreed standards, in every local authority to cater for a minimum of 60% of all 3- and 4-year-olds;

★ within 5 years thereafter, sufficient nursery education places, meeting nationally agreed standards, in every local authority area to cater for 95% of 4-year-olds and 85% of 3-year-olds.

Local reviews of nursery education

We recommend that Education and Training Boards develop and publish plans, no later than 1995, for improving under-5s provision. To identify the amount of improvement needed to meet the targets, the Boards should mount reviews of the availability and quality of services. Wide consultation with providers, including private and voluntary agencies, as well as with members of the public, should be a feature of the reviews.

Under the Children Act 1989, local authorities are already required to carry out three-yearly reviews of their services for young children, taking into account the educational input into any childcare setting. The local reviews which we recommend would build on these arrangements. Co-operation between different departments within local authorities, particularly education, social services and health, will be essential in overcoming fragmented policies and provision. Encouraging progress in this direction is already happening as a result of the Children Act.

Following publication of plans for under-5s provision, it should be the responsibility of Education and Training Boards to secure suitable nursery education places in sufficient numbers and to monitor progress towards local and national targets. Continuing high standards should be promoted through the local and national inspection system which we describe in Chapter 13.

Several issues should receive particular attention in the local reviews:

1 The quality of education offered to under-5s in infant classes in primary schools. For example, what proportion of teachers are trained early years specialists? What is the ratio of adults to children in infant classes? How big are the teaching groups to which children are allocated? Are the needs of 4-year-olds well met by the curriculum, the teaching methods used and the length of the sessions?

2 Priorities which demand targeted resources in the short term. Education and Training Boards should concentrate funding for immediate expansion and improvement on deprived areas, in order to help children living in areas of urban disadvantage or rural isolation. Other needs which might give rise to targeted pre-school provision would include children with special educational needs and children whose mother tongue is not English. The Boards' overall plans for nursery education should take account of their duty under the Children Act 1989 to make provision for individual children identified as being 'in need'.

3 The availability of suitable, affordable daycare and out of school care linked with education. Parental choice of under-5s provision is influenced by ease of access. Some may want a combination of education and care services. Many may, of necessity, opt for whole-daycare arrangements of poor quality because nursery education is part-time. From the point of view of the individual child who may experience both kinds of services in the course of a day or week, a certain continuity of aims and standards between different types of provision is desirable. The extent of co-ordination between care and education services is therefore an important matter, and we note with approval that in several local authorities, all pre-school services are now under the responsibility of the education department. For all these reasons, the availability and quality of daycare facilities, and the identification of requirements for additional public funding, should form part of local reviews.

Some authorities have recognised the value of an integrated approach by setting up combined nursery centres, jointly funded by education and social services departments, offering both daycare and nursery education, often in conjunction with other family support services. By 1990, no more than about 50 such centres existed. Local reviews should consider the benefits of this model in responding to the needs of disadvantaged areas.

Funding

Finally, the issue of funding for improvement must be addressed. Central government funds directed to Education and Training Boards for nursery education should be based on an assessment of the number of 3- and 4-year-olds in the population, the amount of local provision already in existence, and additional needs created by local targets for expansion and improvement. It will not be sufficient to consider the cost of expanding nursery schools and classes: government funding will also be needed to enhance the quality of the educational experience offered in playgroups, nurseries, and for children below compulsory school age in infant classes. The Commission believes that, where insufficient places are available in maintained nursery education, the educational element of playgroup and daycare provision should be free of charge.

The great diversity and unevenness of present provision make it difficult to calculate with any precision how much additional expenditure will be required to achieve the Commission's aims for nursery education. We estimate that to provide nursery education of good quality (whether in nursery schools and classes or in playgroups and daycare settings) to meet our long-term target of provision for 85% of 3-year-olds and 95% of 4-year-olds will eventually require additional annual expenditure of approximately £860 million, excluding capital expenditure. Possible mechanisms for raising education funding for this and other purposes are illustrated in Chapter 14.

To set against expenditure on developing a high-quality education service for under-5s, the Commission stresses the hidden cost of taking no action. We are persuaded that the gains made by children who receive high-quality pre-school education will reduce the need for remedial education at a later stage, help to ensure that we do not waste talent, and perhaps also reduce the social costs which arise from youth unemployment and juvenile crime.

To ensure that Education and Training Boards are locally accountable for their decisions, information about the amount of central government funds passed to the Boards for nursery education purposes should be made public.

The issue of daycare funding is not part of the Commission's remit, except in respect of improving the quality of the educational component of care. We recognise that there is considerable unmet demand for daycare and out-of-school care for young children. We note that, in 1991, the National Children's Bureau claimed that a fourfold expansion in daycare places was required. The Commission's view is that high-quality daycare should receive public subsidy, and that parents should pay for it according to their means.

Through national and local commitment to improved standards, coupled with short- and long-term targets for expansion in provision, we can begin to make progress towards three goals: giving every child the opportunity of a good foundation for learning; removing inequalities in provision across the country; and bringing the UK into line with the levels of pre-school services offered in many other parts of the European Community.

Notes

1   Department for Education, March 1993. Questions Addressed to the Department for Education by the NCE. A Note by DFE.

2   Pugh, G., November 1992. *An Equal Start for All Our Children?* The Second Times Educational Supplement/Greenwich Lecture.

3   Keys, W. and Fernandes, C., 1993. *What Do Students Think About School?* A Report for the National Commission on Education. National Foundation for Educational Research, Part II, p. 12.

4   Cohen, B. and Fraser, N., 1991. *Childcare in a Modern Welfare System. Towards a New National Policy*. Institute for Public Policy Research.

5   Mortimore, P. and others, 1988. *School Matters*, Open Books.

6   Osborn, A. F. and Millbank, J.E., 1987. *The Effects of Early Education*. A Report from the Child Health and Education Study. Oxford University Press.

7   Jowett, S and Sylva, K., 1986. *'Does Kind of Pre-School Matter?'* Educational Research, 28 (1), 21-31.

8   Athey, C., 1990. *Extending Thought in Young Children*. Paul Chapman Publishing.

9   Consortium of Longitudinal Studies, 1983. *As the Twig is Bent: Lasting Effects of Pre-School Programmes*. Lawrence Erlbaum Associates.

10 Schweinhart, L. J. and Weikart, D. P., 1993. *A Summary of 'Significant Benefits: the High/Scope Perry Preschool Study through Age 27'*. High/Scope UK.

11 Utting, D. and others, June 1993. *Crime and the Family. Improving Child-Rearing and Preventing Delinquency*. Family Policy Studies Centre Occasional Paper 16.

12 Pugh, G., op cit.

13 Howes, C., 1990. *'Can the Age of Entry into Child Care and the Quality of Child Care Predict Adjustment in Kindergarten?'* Developmental Psychology, 26 (2), pp. 292-303.

14 Sylva K. and others, 1992. *'The Impact of the UK National Curriculum on Pre-School Practice: Some 'Top Down' Processes at Work.'* International Journal of Early Education, 24, pp. 40-53.

15 House of Commons Education, Science and Arts Committee, January 1989. *Educational Provision for the Under Fives.* HMSO.

16 Holtermann, S., 1992. *Investing in Young Children. Costing an Education and Daycare Service.* National Children's Bureau Early Childhood Unit.

17 Ibid.

18 Cohen, B. and Fraser, N., 1991, op cit.

19 Employers for Childcare, May 1993. *Good Childcare, Good Business.*

20 Government Statistical Service, 1993. *Education Statistics for United Kingdom.* 1992 Edition, Table B page 4 and notes.

21 Sources: England Department for Education. Statistical Bulletin 11/93, May 1993.

　　　　　　　Wales: Welsh Office. Pupil count as at January 1992. Ages as at 31 December 1991.

　　　　　　　Scotland: Scottish Office Education Department. School Census September 1991.

　　　　　　　Northern Ireland: Department of Education. Pupil count as at January 1992. Ages as at December 1991.

　　　Note variation in pupil count between countries.

22 See: (i)   Statistics of Education and Training in Wales: Schools. No. 1 1993. Table 2.04.

　　　　　(ii)   Department for Education, Statistical Bulletin 11/93. Pupils Under Five Years of Age in Schools in England – January 1992.

23 Sources:

　　(i)   England: Based on: Department for Education. Statistical Bulletin 11/93. May 1993.

　　(ii) Wales: Welsh Office. Pupil count as at January 1992. Ages as at 31 December 1991. Population figures are provisional mid-year estimates for June 1991.

　　(iii) Scotland: Scottish Office Education Department. School Census September 1991. General Register for Scotland mid-1991 population estimates.

　　(iv) Northern Ireland: Department for Education. Pupil count as at January 1992. Ages as at December 1991. Age breakdown of pupils in nursery classes estimated according to the split in nursery schools. Government Actuary Department mid-1991 population estimates between countries.

24 See 2(ii).

25 Woodhead, M., 1989. *'School Starts at Five … or Four Years Old? The Rationale for Changing Admission Policies in England and Wales.'* Journal of Education Policy, 4 (1), pp. 1-21.

26 Ibid.

27 Her Majesty's Inspectorate, 1989. *Aspects of Primary Education.* The Education of Children Under Five. HMSO.

28 Pascal, C., 1990. *Under Fives in the Infant Classroom.* Trentham Books.

29 HMI, 1992. Education in England 1990-91. The Annual Report of HM Senior Chief Inspector of Schools. Department of Education and Science.

30 Woodhead, M., 1989, op cit.

31 Sylva, K. and Moss, P., November 1992. *Learning before School.* NCE Briefing No. 8. National Commission on Education.

32 Ibid, Table 1.

33 Holtermann, S., 1992, op cit.

34 House of Commons Education, Science and Arts Committee, 1989, op cit.

35 Holtermann, S., 1992, op cit.

36 Committee of Inquiry into the Quality of the Educational Experience Offered to 3- and 4-year-Olds, chaired by Mrs Angela Rumbold CBE MP, 1990. *Starting with Quality.* HMSO.

37. Ibid.

38 Ibid.

Early Learning: Suggested Reading

It is hoped that this list will be helpful to the non-specialist lay reader; it is not intended for 'experts' in early childhood education who have access to excellent bibliographies.

Government reports and other papers

Department of Education and Science. (1989). *Aspects of Primary Education: the education of children under five*, London: HMI Report.

Education, Science and Arts Committee. (1986). *Achievement in Primary Schools*, Vols. 1 & 2. London: HMSO.

Education, Science and Arts Committee. (1988). *Educational Provision for the Under Fives*, Vols 1 & 2. London: HMSO.

Department of Education and Science. (1990). *Starting with Quality*. The Rumbold Report of the Committee of Inquiry into the Quality of the Educational Experience offered to 3- and 4-year-olds. London: HMSO.

Rathbone, T. (MP). (1990). *Nursery Schooling: too long the overlooked ingredient in education for life*. Tory Reform Group.

Taylor, A. (Shadow Secretary of State for Education) *Start to Build; stop the rot*. A consultative green paper on education. Labour Party.

Policy and resources

Association of Metropolitan Authorities. (1991). *Children First*: Report of the AMA Working Party on Services to Young Children

Brophy, J., Statham, J. & Moss, P. (1992). *Playgroups in practice: self-help and public policy*. London: HMSO.

Bruner, J. (1980) *Under Five in Britain*, London: McIntyre/Blackwell.

Equal Opportunities Commission. (1990). *The key to real choice*. An action plan for childcare, discussion paper. Manchester.

Holtermann, S. (1992). *Investing in Young Children: costing an education and daycare service*, London: National Children's Bureau.

Moss, P. (1988). *Childcare and equality of opportunity*. European Commission Childcare Network.

Moss, P. (1990). *Childcare in the European Community 1985-1990*. European Commission Childcare Network.

Moss, P., Brophy, J., Statham, J. (forthcoming). 'Poor relations in the pre-school family: the funding of playgroups'. *Journal of Education Policy*, 7 (5), pp. 471-491.

Owen, C. & Moss, P. (1989). 'Patterns of pre-school provision in English local authorities'. *Journal of Education Policy*, 4, pp. 309-328.

Pugh, G. (1988) *Services for Under Fives: developing a coordinated approach*, London: National Children's Bureau.

Pugh, G (Ed.). (1992). *Contemporary issues in the early years: working collaboratively with children*. London: National Children's Bureau and Paul Chapman Publishers Ltd.

Sylva, K. & Moss, P. (1992). *Learning Before School*. Briefings, National Commission on Education. London: Heinemann.

Skilbeck, M. (1993). The utility of early childhood education: an OECD view. *European Early Childhood Education Research Journal*, Vol. 1 (1), p.5-16.

Watt, J. (1990). *Early Education: the current debate*. Scottish Academic Press.

Early Years' curriculum and assessment

Bennett, N. & Kell, C.L. (1989). *A good start? Four year olds in infant schools*. Oxford: Blackwell Education.

Bertram, A. & Pascal, C (forthcoming) *Developing a Quality Curriculum for Young Children*

Blenkin, G. & Kelly, A.V. (Eds.). (1988). *Early childhood education: a developmental curriculum*. London: Paul Chapman Publishing Ltd.

Blenkin, G. & Kelly, A.V. (1992) *Assessment in Early Childhood Education*, London: Paul Chapman Publishing Ltd.

Browne, N. (Ed.). (1990). *Science and Technology in the Early Years. An equal opportunities approach*. Open University Press.

Bruce, T. (1991). *Time to Play in Early Childhood Education*, Hodder & Stoughton.

Clay, M. (1991). *Becoming Literate: the Construction of Inner Control*, Auckland: Heinemann.

Curtis, A. (1986) *A Curriculum for the Preschool Child*, NFER Nelson.

David, T. (1991). *Under five – under educated*. England: Open University.

DesForges, C. (Ed.). (1989) 'Early Childhood Education' *British Journal of Educational Psychology* Monograph, 4, Scottish Press.

Dowling, M. (1992) *Education 3-5*. London: Paul Chapman Publishing Ltd.

Drummond, M., Rouse, D. & Pugh, G. (1992) *Making Assessment Work: values and principles in assessing young children's learning*, NCB/NES Arnold.

Early Years Curriculum Group (1989) *Early Childhood Education*, Staffordshire: Trentham Books Limited.

Gammage, P. and Meighan, J. *Early Childhood Education: Taking Stock*. Education Now.

Groswami, U. & Bryant, P. (1990) *Phonological Skills and Learning to Read*. Lawrence Erlbaum Ltd.

Heath, S.B. (1983). *Ways with Words*. New York: Cambridge University Press.

Hohmann, M., Banet, B. & Weikart, D. (1979) *Young Children in Action*, The High/Scope Press.

Hughes, M. (1986). *Children and number. Difficulties in learning mathematics*. Oxford: Basil Blackwell Ltd.

Hurst, V. (1991). *Planning for early learning and education in the first five years*. London: Paul Chapman Publishing Ltd.

Lally, M. (1991) *The Nursery Teacher in Action*. London: Paul Chapman Publishing Ltd.

Meek, M. (1988) *How Texts Teach What Readers Learn*, Stroud: Thimble Press.

Paley, V. G. (1981). *Wally's Stories*. Cambridge (Mass): Harvard University Press.

Porter, R. (1988) *Computers and Learning in the First Years of School*, Social Science Press, Australia.

Spodek, B. & Saracho, O. (1990) 'Early Curriculum Construction and Classroom Practice', *Early Child Development and Care*, Vol 61, pp.1-11.

Sylva, K. (1991) 'Educational Aspects of Day Care', in E. Melhuish and P. Moss, (Eds). *Day Care for Young Children*. HMSO Department of Health.

Wells, G. (1987) *The Meaning Makers: Children Learning Language and using Language to learn*, London: Hodder and Stoughton.

Child development

Athey, C. (1990). *Extending thought in young children: a parent-teacher partnership*. London: Paul Chapman Publishing Ltd.

Bruner, J. & Haste, H. (Eds.) (1987) *Making Sense*. London: Methuen.

Bruner, J.S., Jolly, A. & Sylva, K. (Eds.). (1976). *Play: Its role in development and evolution*. Penguin Books.

Donaldson, M. (1978). *Children's Minds*. London: Fontana.

Dunn, J. (1988). *The Beginning of Social Understanding*. Oxford: Blackwell.

Hartup, W. & Rubin, Z. (Eds.). (1986). *Relationships and Development*. Hillsdale (NY): Lawrence Erlbaum.

Henshall, C. & McGuire, J. (1986). 'Gender Development' in M. Richards and P. Light. (Eds.), *Children of Social Worlds* (pp. 135-167). London: Cambridge University Press.

Light, P., Sheldon, S. & Woodhead, M. (Eds.). (1991). *Learning to Think; Child Development in Social Context*. Open University, Routledge.

Wood, D. (1988) *How Children Think and Learn*. Oxford: Basil Blackwell Ltd.

Parental involvement

Hewison, J. & Tizard, J. (1980). Parental involvement and reading attainment. *British Journal of Educational Psychology*, Vol 50, pp.209-215.

Hewison, J. (1988). The long term effectiveness of parental involvement in reading: a follow up to the Haringey Reading Project. *British Journal of Educational Psychology*, Vol 58, pp.184-190.

Jowett, S., Baginsky, M. & MacDonald, M. (1991). *Building bridges: parental involvement in schools*. Windsor: NFER-Nelson.

Pugh, G. & De'Ath, E. (1989). *Working towards partnership in the early years*, London: National Children's Bureau.

Wolfendale, S. (Ed.). (1989). *Parental Involvement*. Croom Helm .

Equal opportunities and cultural diversity

Biggs, A.P., Edwards, A.V. (1992). *'I treat them all the same'. Teacher-pupil talk in multi-ethnic classrooms*. Vol. 5 (3), pp. 161-176.

Brown, N. & France, P. (Eds.). (1986). *Untying the apron strings*. Milton Keynes: Open University Press.

Derman-Sparks, L. (1989). *Anti-bias curriculum. Tools for empowering young children*. Washington: NAECE.

Pinsent, P. (Ed.). (1992). *Language, culture and young children*. Fulton.

Pugh, G. (1992). *An equal start for all our children?*. London: National Children's Bureau.

Siraj-Blatchford, I. (1994). *The early years. Laying the foundations for racial equality*. Staffordshire: Trentham Books.

Training of teachers and other workers

Association for teacher education in Europe. (1991). *Comparative directory of initial training*. ATEE, The Association of Teacher Education in Europe Early Years Working Group.

Early Childhood Unit. (1992). *The future of training on the early years*. London: National Children's Bureau.

Evaluation and research

(see referrals in appendix C).

Attachment (Bowlby) and out-of-home care

Belsky, J. (1988). 'The effects of infant day care reconsidered'. *Early Childhood Research Quarterly*, **3**, pp. 235-272.

Belsky, J. & Braungart, J. (1991). 'Are insecure avoidant infants with extensive day-care experience less stressed by and more independent in the Strange Situation?'. *Child Development*, 62, pp. 567-571.

Bowlby, J. (1982). *Attachment*. (2nd Edition of Vol. 1 of *Attachment and Loss*). London: Hogarth Press.

Bowlby, J. (1988). *A secure base: clinical application of attachment theory*. London: Routledge.

Clark-Stewart, A. (1991). 'Infant day care: maligned or malignant?' in M. Woodhead, P. Light and R. Carr (Eds), *Growing up in a changing society*. London and New York: The Open University, Routledge.

McGurk, H., Caplan, M., Hennessy, E. & Moss, P. (1993). 'Controversy, theory and social context in contemporary day care research'. *Journal of Child Psychology and Psychiatry*, 34 (1), pp. 3-24.

Schaffer, R. (1990). *Making decisions about children: psychological decisions and answers*. Basil Blackwell.

Tizard, B. (1986). *The care of young children; implications of recent research*. Thomas Coram Research Unit; Working and Occasional Papers, pp. 331-348.